How to Sell on

Begginer to Advanced

Detailed Guide on How to Sell to Make Money.
What Items to List, Where to Source, How to Ship, Tips to
Increase Sales, Business Hacks and More.

By

Queen Thrift

Connect with me on Instagram:
@queen_thrift1 or scan below

SCAN ME

Facebook: https://www.facebook.com/QueenThriftOriginal/

Pin me on Pinterest:
https://**www.pinterest.com/queenthrift1/_created/**

Dedicado A Mi Papá,
Domingo Hector del Rosario

Por su insistencia en la lectura, la cultura, y el aprendizaje,
soy la persona que soy hoy.

Gracias papá por todo.
Te quiero,

Geludys Aleska del Rosario

Contents

Introduction

Welcome to the world of eBay business! The resale market has exploded in recent years, with online platforms like eBay at the head of this growth. According to a study by Forbes*, in 2022, the resale market was valued at 119 billion dollars and is expected to reach $218 billion by 2026. A 127% increase in the next three years!

According to the same study by Forbes*, "The worldwide second-hand clothing market is growing 11 times faster than traditional retail". With more and more people turning to online shopping and a growing interest in sustainable living, now is the perfect time to start an eBay business.

Starting an eBay business allows you to tap into the vast and lucrative world of online sales and enables you to work from home and be your boss. Whether you're looking to supplement your income or replace your full-time job, eBay offers the perfect opportunity to become an entrepreneur.

This book will guide you to start your eBay business from scratch. You will learn how to set up your eBay account, source inventory, create attractive listings and provide the best customer service.

---

* https://www.forbes.com/sites/catherineerdly/2021/06/27/the-resale-market-is-booming-heres-how-small-businesses-can-benefit/?sh=101a04197c62

We'll cover everything you need to know to succeed in your eBay business. Plus, with eBay's vast audience and built-in features, you don't need to worry about building a website or investing in an expensive physical (brick-and-mortar) store.

So whether you're an experienced entrepreneur or a complete beginner, this book will give you the tools and knowledge you need to start and grow a successful eBay business in 2023 and beyond.

What you will Learn
in this book:

This book represents a comprehensive guide that you can go back to and use as a reference. Each chapter has guidance, principles, best practices, examples, and my personal experience.

From the beginning, you will learn how to sell on eBay to advanced techniques for experienced sellers. From opening your first eBay store, setting your payment options, getting things to sell, how to sell, how to ship it, and how to provide customer service.

Even how to deal with the most common disputes you can encounter when dealing with customers.

Some of the things you will learn inside:

- I break down every part of a listing and go over each step in detail. I offer best practices, pro tips, and strategies for your title, description, and best shipping options.

- You get a list of the most popular and profitable categories to sell in. These should get you started in looking for the right items to sell.

- List of where to find items to fill your store. Some sources may surprise you.

- I share my tips and tricks for getting more money for your items, visibility, fewer fees, and more efficiency in your processes.

- I explain how to ship your items correctly, cut costs, and do it more efficiently.

- I will explain eBay fees and give you tips on reducing them.

- Learn one of the most critical aspects of selling on eBay, how to take great photos that sell themselves.

- How to use eBay's marketing tools to make your listing stand out.

At the end of the book, you will be ready to put into practice all the principles and techniques you have learned and start listing your first few items. There is no better way to learn than by doing.

Being an entrepreneur is only a dream to some. But for those who put in the work, it is a reality.

Some Considerations Before Your Start Your eBay Journey

Starting an eBay business is an excellent method to work for yourself and generate a sizable income. Yet it's crucial to realize that this isn't a get-rich-quick plan. Like any other business, eBay needs time, effort, and hard work to succeed.

We'll discuss several tips for someone establishing an eBay business in this chapter, such as the value of perseverance and the advantages of working for yourself.

Understand that Success Takes Time and Effort

You must invest time and energy in researching items to sell, sourcing inventory, creating attractive listings, and providing the best customer service. Do not expect to become an eBay millionaire overnight.

You will need time to go through many sales and make a few mistakes to grasp how to run this business. The trick is to learn from those mistakes, not make them again, and learn something new daily.

Also, try to improve every day in different areas of your business. Learn new ways to do inventory, sourcing, shipping, etc. The more you learn, the more money you will make.

This book will give you the tools you need to succeed. However, it's up to you to put in the work and be patient enough to create a profitable business.

Set Realistic Goals

To succeed, you must set realistic goals for your business. Start by determining how much time and energy you can devote to your eBay business. Then, set achievable goals for your sales, revenue, and growth. Setting realistic goals will help you stay motivated and focused and avoid burnout or disappointment.

Focus on Customer Service

You must provide excellent customer service to build a successful eBay business. To do this, you must promptly respond to customer inquiries, ship orders quickly and accurately, and resolve any issues or concerns. Happy customers are likelier to leave positive feedback, recommend your business to others, and become repeat customers. Make sure that customer service is a top priority for your eBay business.

Stay Educated and Informed

E-commerce trends and best practices are constantly changing, so keeping up with what's happening is essential. Reading blogs and articles, attending webinars and conferences, and networking with other eBay sellers are great ways to do this.

By staying informed, you'll be better prepared to adapt and make informed business decisions. It's important to understand that success takes time, effort, and dedication.

By setting realistic goals, focusing on customer service, and staying educated and informed, you can build a thriving eBay business that supports your financial and personal goals.

Is eBay Passive Income?

If you have been perusing YouTube, you may have heard the term "Passive income" however, there is a quote that I suggest you write it down on a piece of paper and keep where you can see it every day:

"There is no passive income without active effort."

The phrase means that people who earn passive income have put in a significant amount of time, effort, and resources upfront to create something of value that can continue to generate revenue over time, like a well-built and well-stocked eBay store.

While passive income can be a great way to supplement your income and build wealth over time, it's important to remember that it typically requires hard work and dedication upfront. Once you have systems, you can reduce your work hours while increasing your income.

The potential benefits of earning passive income - including increased financial freedom, flexibility, and the ability to earn money while you sleep - make it a worthwhile investment of your time and resources.

Chapter 1.
Set up Your eBay Business.

Whether you're a seasoned business owner or starting, eBay is an incredible platform to expand your reach and find new customers. But before diving headfirst into listing items and making sales, setting up your eBay account correctly is crucial to ensure you can receive payments and conduct transactions smoothly.

Setting up an eBay business account can seem overwhelming, especially if you're new. But don't worry - we're here to guide you through every step of the way!

In the following sections, we'll dive deeper into each step and provide tips and best practices to make the process as smooth and stress-free as possible. By the end of this chapter, you'll be equipped with the knowledge you need to start selling on eBay confidently. So let's get started!

Step 1: Go to eBay.com and click on "register"

The first step to selling on eBay is to create an account. Visit eBay.com and click on the "register" button in the top left corner of the page.

Step 2: Provide your personal information

To create your eBay account, you must provide your personal information, such as your name, address, phone number, and email address.

Use an email address you frequently check, as eBay will send important information about your account to that email.

Step 3: Create a username and password

Next, you must choose a username and password for your eBay account. Your username will be the name buyers see when they view your listings, so choose something easy to remember and professional. Your password should be strong and secure to prevent unauthorized access to your account.

Step 4: Setup your payment account

eBay requires sellers to have a checking account to receive payments. Once you login into your account, go to "My eBay" and click on "Account" then "Payment options."

Step 5: Set up your seller account

To start selling, you need to set up your seller account. Go to "My eBay" and click on "Account," then "Seller Hub." From there, you can choose to open either a business account or a personal account.

Essential tips when opening an eBay account:

- Create an email address to use just for your reselling business. You can get a free one with Gmail. It is the best email service for businesses; you get plenty of storage on their google cloud drive. I use this drive to store my photos for easy download to my computer for listing.

  Create all accounts related to buying and selling using this email address. Apps can and will miss notifications. An email address dedicated to your business will keep you updated with your eBay store.

- When choosing an eBay store name, choose one that correlates to the items you plan to sell. If you are still determining what you will sell, select a name that sounds professional and easy to remember.

  Choose something catchy that you can use with a wide variety of items. You can always change this later.

- You don't have to sign up for a store immediately when you first start. However, I highly recommend you do, even if it's the Basic or the Starter store. You will get many more features like analytics, marketing tools, and free shipping supplies.

- Get the phone app. Download the version your phone supports and start getting familiar with it. You can list and edit items and send offers and answers to customers' emails.

Supplies You Will Need

Like any other business, you will need some basic supplies to start. In the beginning, avoid purchasing any costly equipment. Please keep it simple until you learn more about running this business, and then consider what can be a good investment in the future.

Here are the basic supplies you will need to start your eBay business:

1. Weight Scale. I recommend getting one with a 50lb (23 kg) limit. You do not need anything fancier than that. Getting one that uses a USB cable to connect to your computer without using batteries is helpful. Buy a new one from a fellow reseller on eBay.com if you can.

2. If you are going to sell clothing, get a simple measuring tape to provide measurements with your listings.

3. Shipping tape. eBay or Amazon offer great deals on this.

4. Boxes and poly mailers. You can get boxes for free just by asking local shops. Please make sure they are clean and in good shape. Poly Mailers are great for shipping simple clothing and soft things like stuffed animals and blankets.

5. Computer or Smartphone for listing and taking pictures. You can entirely run your eBay business from your phone.

Nowadays, phones have great cameras that can take great pictures. You can list your items with the eBay app and use a wireless printer to print your labels.

6. Get a regular printer or thermal label printer to print your shipping labels.

    If you cannot access a printer, weigh and measure your packages correctly, then use the free computer time at the library or your local college to print your shipping labels. Then tape the labels to your parcel and take it to the Post Office.

7. You will need spare batteries to test electronics and toys.

These basic supplies should get you started.

You will add the necessary tools and supplies as you become more experienced in your eBay business. Cleaning pads, sprays, and lint-free cloth to clean electronics are supplies you will need to get later.

How to Setup your eBay Store

Think about what kind of store you want to have. Are you going to sell primarily vintage? Athletic wear? Tools and equipment? A little bit of everything?

There are two eBay business models that you can adopt, and it all depends on your goals.

If you are more of a "Hobby Seller" and want to make extra money by selling items you enjoy shopping for, then the "A little bit of everything" business model will work for you.

If you plan to resell full-time, you need to invest more time in planning your store and the items you will sell.

You will benefit from having a niched-down store. However, it's worth exploring both.

"Little bit of Everything" Business Model

When you start, you should sell items you already have around the house. Think of it like a garage sale store, which is perfectly fine when you first start. These items will give you experience with how things work in the e-commerce world.

I know many sellers who have this store model and make a good living doing it; it just takes many more items and time.

Here are the pros and cons of this business model:

Pros

- You can easily find $10 to $20 profit items in any thrift store across many product categories.

- Since you are not strictly loyal to any category, you can sell anything you can profit from, expanding the type of items you can offer in your eBay store.

- Learning about different items and categories is a good learning experience.

Cons

- Few repeat customers. A person who bought an umbrella from you may not return for a pair of pants.

- Unless you already know them, you must research most (if not all) of the items you get. You are making listing items a slow process.

- Shipping can take longer since you have to accommodate the various sizes, breakability, customer requests, carriers, etc. It's hard to have every shipping supply you need, the perfect box, poly mailer, etc.

- You risk looking unprofessional. Buyers like to deal with sellers who are experts in what they sell. If your store is full of random items, you may need to give more confidence to a new buyer that you know what you're doing.

- Inventory can be hard to manage. Accommodating the growing number of odd items you plan to sell, storing them can create a challenge. You will need to create an inventory system to keep track of all your items. The last thing you want is to spend hours looking for just one item, lowering your hourly rate.

- Since you are not catering to a specific audience, you will need many items to make your store profitable. And having so much inventory can break your cash flow and put you out of business. Be careful with your spending.

The "Niche Store" Model

As you gain experience selling different types of items, you will notice that you are better at selling some things than others.

At one point, I was selling much clothing. Because so much was available near me, I enjoyed buying and selling it, and customers liked what I was listing.

However, it started to get draining and overwhelming. The piles were piling up, and it just got to a point where I could not manage to keep up with the listings. I decided to research other types of items that I could sell, list quicker, sell quicker, and keep things moving out.

Note: If you decide to sell clothing items (which is a great way to start, by the way, since you already own clothing items that you can begin to list immediately), know that they can be very long tail (long term), which means that clothing can sit in your store for a long time before the right buyer comes along.

Some items like suits, party dresses, and wedding attire can take a year or more to sell. So, you will be hanging on to the clothing a lot longer. The upside is that it is a lot available, and as you learn popular brands and styles, you too can carve yourself a niche in this category. Just know that you must establish a remarkably efficient inventory system early to keep up with your inventory. More on this later on in the book.

While researching different items I was interested in selling, I found the toy niche—specifically vintage and newer dolls like barbies and American Girl. I was so hooked! I sought to learn all that I could about them. And as I was doing that, I devised ways to source them near me.

I posted on all the local Facebook buy/sell groups advertising that I was buying dolls and posted the brands and models I was looking to buy. I hit up yard sales, state sales, and thrift stores and purchased from the (Facebook) marketplace from local people. I began to be known as the "crazy doll lady" in my area (true story).

I now have an eBay store specializing in those types of dolls. I sell everything from repair kits to handmade clothing, accessories, dolls, books, pamphlets, and more under the doll category.

My store looks uniform and professional, and I get repeat buyers that come to my store to shop regularly.

Pros of this model:

- Customer feedback has been overwhelmingly positive. Many seek discontinued items, parts, dolls, and the like.

  I have repeat customers that visit my shop every week and buy. That is how you build a successful store. Build relationships with repeat customers who keep coming to your store for more.

- Stores specializing in a few related niches or categories are more sustainable over time. As you become an expert in your area, you can identify these high-value items quicker when buying inventory.

- You can list items much quicker because you know their value, how to describe them, and what customers need to know about your item.

- Sourcing for these items is easier because you know what you are looking for, what you expect to pay for them, and in what condition they need to be in for you to make a profit.

- You can build a network of buyers and sellers in your local area. Posting ads on your local bulletin boards (Facebook, craigslist, offer up, etc.) can bring you items instead of you going out to look for them.

When buying from others, keep accurate records and provide receipts.

Even after you specialize in a few categories, it's always a good idea to have experience selling various items. It will teach you what things sell faster, for more money, and what to purchase locally to keep reselling.

Listing various items will also help you determine what you enjoy buying, listing, and selling. After all, if you are going to be spending time growing this business, you should be enjoying yourself.

Finding those items that sell well for you and that you have fun doing is the perfect combination. Remember that getting good at anything takes time; have patience and keep learning.

How to Craft a Great Brand Customers Will Love

As your store grows and you gain experience, you need to start thinking about creating a brand for your store. A brand is nothing more than an identity for your business. A name that others can use to identify what you offer. For example, names like Coca-Cola and Pepsi are brands that the whole world recognizes.

A strong brand can help differentiate your products and services from your competitors, build trust with your customers, and create an emotional connection that keeps them returning for more.

But creating a great brand isn't just about clever marketing campaigns or catchy slogans - it's about staying true to your values and standing behind your products.

If you are not proud of what you are selling, chances are buyers will be hesitant to buy from your store, and your items will end up sitting for a while.

Let's explore the critical elements of successful branding and show you how to create a brand that resonates with your customers and reflects your company's unique personality and mission.

- **Engage with Your Customers**
  Building a solid brand requires engaging with your customers regularly. Respond to customer inquiries and reviews promptly and with empathy. Use social media to create a two-way conversation with your customers, ask for feedback and suggestions, and promptly respond to comments and messages. Practicing this will help build brand loyalty and create a community around your business.

- **Develop a Memorable Logo**
  Your logo visually represents your brand and should be memorable and easily recognizable. It should also be consistent across all marketing materials, including your eBay store, social media accounts, business cards, and communications. Consider hiring a graphic designer to create a professional and visually appealing logo, or use an online logo maker if you're on a budget.

- **Use Consistent Branding Elements**
  Consistency is vital when it comes to creating a memorable brand. Use consistent branding elements across all marketing materials, such as colors, fonts, and imagery. Keeping all your communications uniform can create a cohesive and recognizable brand identity that customers will remember.

- **Display Your Brand Proudly**
  Order supplies with your brand colors and logo as soon as your budget allows. You can apply your brand to anything from poly mailers to packing material and postcards.

- Consider including a **thank you card** with all your orders as a courtesy. These cards provide an incentive, such as a discount on their next order. If they had a good experience the first time buying from you, they would most likely do it again.

You can easily create a thank you card using Canva or other graphic software. If you are not design-inclined, you can head to Etsy and buy a template for just a few dollars. You can then customize the template, send it to a printer, and have your cards ready to include with your shipment.

Many online companies (Google Search) will print your cards very inexpensively. Keep records of your purchases in your ledger, as you can deduct this expense come tax time.

Display your brand in all your communications, social media, listings, and shipments. It's a great way to incite confidence in your buyers and bring you those repeat sales.

Some Branding Budget Ideas:

- Use free design tools like Canva to create marketing materials such as flyers, social media graphics, and business cards.

- Opt for cost-effective printing options like Vistaprint or local print shops.

- Host a launch event or pop-up shop in a low-cost location like a community center or local market.

- Use social media to your advantage: social media is a powerful tool for engaging with customers and building brand loyalty. In addition to posting regular updates and responding to comments

- Collaborate with other small businesses or influencers in your community for mutually beneficial marketing opportunities.

- Use word-of-mouth marketing by encouraging satisfied customers to refer their friends and family to your business.

Creating a memorable brand for your small business requires a clear understanding of your brand identity, consistency in branding elements, a strong brand voice, telling your brand story, and engaging with your customers.

With these tips and budget-friendly ideas, you can create a solid and recognizable brand to help your business stand out and thrive.

Should you sign up for the store subscription?

When you first join eBay, you automatically get some free listings. Depending on what eBay sets as the minimum, usually ten at the time of printing, you will have those free listings to start posting items for sale.

Your limit should increase as your feedback grows and you get some sales. You can continue to list on eBay without a subscription if you want to list just a few items a month.

If you want to sell some items you no longer use or sell as a hobby, the free account will work for you. However, you must immediately subscribe to the store model to make eBay a legit business.

Benefits of Signing up for the Store Subscription:

- 250 Free listings minimum every month. Zero insertion fees, meaning you can list for free.

- Lower final value fees (fees you pay when you sell your item, based on the item's total price. See the chapter on costs.

- Access to special reports and metrics. Helpful insight into how your store is doing: traffic, impressions, visitors, etc.

- Branding. You get your custom URL (ebay.com/your-storename). Display your custom banner and logo in your eBay store.

- Free eBay branded shipping supplies. Every three months, you will get a coupon for $25 to spend on the eBay shipping store. Get boxes, tape, envelopes, and more.

- Discount on services like printing, shipping, eBay store customization, accounting services, and more.

Which Store Subscription Should You Choose?

I always recommend you start with the "Starter" plan. At the time of printing, you get 250 free listings, along with reduced fees. You will not get the shipping supplies coupon or the discounts on services (which you will not need immediately).

Two hundred fifty free listings are enough to get you started listing some items, processing some sales, and getting a feel for what eBay is and how it works.

Remember that when you start, you want to gather items you own to sell online. You want to figure out how things work and possibly make some mistakes with regular items that can easily list and ship quickly.

Later, when you have grown your store past the 250 items or want to start using the advanced eBay tools, sign up for the next tier. The "Basic Store." This one will give you a lot more tools (later in the book) that you can use to gauge how your store is doing, what you can do to improve, and what you have to stop doing (or buying).

Initially, it is best to concentrate on selling items rather than over-whelm yourself with the gadgets and numbers that eBay gives you when you dive into them.

Focus on learning how the eBay business works and developing systems to improve your listing routine's efficiency.

Should You Register Your Business Right Away?

Please note that this does not constitute legal or tax advice. You need to consult with a tax professional in your local area who can advise you on these issues. So please consult a tax/ attorney professional.

Registering your business with the local government has both advantages and disadvantages. On the one hand, registering your business makes it legitimate, giving you access to certain benefits and protections. For example, registered companies may be eligible for government grants and loans. They can secure financing more easily than unregistered businesses.

Additionally, registering your business can give you legal protection, making it easier to protect your intellectual property and defend against lawsuits.

However, registering your business also comes with some potential downsides. For one, registering your business can be time-consuming and expensive, with fees for filing paperwork and obtaining permits varying by location. Additionally, registered companies are subject to specific regulations and requirements, such as annual reporting and compliance with local tax laws.

Another potential disadvantage of registering your business is the loss of privacy. Once you register your business, your information will be publicly available, which could expose you to unwanted attention or solicitations from unwanted sources.

Overall, the decision to register your business with the local government is a personal one and depends on your specific needs and goals as a new business owner. While registration can offer many benefits, it also comes with its challenges, so it's essential to carefully weigh the pros and cons before deciding.

Like any other business, you must ensure you follow the laws where you live. A simple Google search can bring up information on how to run a business in your area.

Ensure the information you get is from official sources, and follow up by calling or visiting the offices where you can ask more questions.

Taxes for Resellers

If you're a reseller residing in the USA, it's essential to understand how taxes work for your business. While tax laws can be complex and vary by state, here are some general recommendations to help you get started.

As a reseller, you are generally not required to pay sales tax on the products you purchase for resale. Instead, you will need to obtain a resale certificate from your state's taxing authority, which allows you to make tax-free purchases for resale purposes. When you sell these products to your customers, you typically charge them sales tax based on location.

It's important to note that sales tax rates vary widely by state and may even vary within a state based on local jurisdictions. Additionally, some states require online marketplaces to collect and remit sales tax on behalf of their sellers. In contrast, others require individual sellers to handle tax collection and reporting.

eBay is a marketplace where they collect the sales tax from all your sales and remit them to your local tax authority on your behalf. To provide that service to you as a reseller, the additional 0.30 cents you pay on your final value fee covers this expense.

To comply with tax laws, it's essential to keep accurate records of your sales and purchases and to stay up-to-date on any changes to tax laws in your state. Consider consulting with a tax professional or accountant to ensure you meet all your tax obligations and take advantage of any available deductions or credits.

Taxes can be a complex and confusing aspect of running a reselling business on an online platform in the USA and the world. However, by understanding your obligations and staying organized, you can ensure you comply with all relevant tax laws and regulations.

USA Reseller Income Threshold

At the end of the year, eBay and any other selling platform will issue a tax document known as the 1099K, which you will use to file your taxes. However, the IRS will not receive the form if you sell under a certain amount or number of sales. This threshold determines when an online platform must issue a 1099-K form to you for tax reporting purposes.

The reseller sales threshold is based on the number of transactions you have completed and the total dollar amount of those transactions. Specifically, suppose you have completed more than 200 transactions and generated more than USD$20,000 in sales through an online platform in a given tax year. In that case, the platform must issue a 1099-K to you and the IRS.

It's important to note that the reseller sales threshold applies to gross sales, meaning the total amount of money you receive from selling goods before any fees or expenses are removed. Additionally, the threshold applies to all transactions, regardless of whether they are taxable or non-taxable.

When you receive a 1099-K from an online platform, the form will report the gross sales generated through the platform and any fees or expenses deducted. You must register this information on your tax return and may be required to pay taxes on your generated income.

It's essential to keep accurate records of your sales and expenses throughout the year to ensure you are prepared to report your income and expenses on your tax return. **Consider consulting with a tax professional or accountant to ensure you meet all your tax obligations and take advantage of any available deductions or credits.**

The reseller sales threshold imposed by the IRS determines when online platforms must issue a 1099-K to resellers for tax reporting purposes. Understanding this threshold and staying organized ensures you comply with all relevant tax laws and regulations.

Even if you do not meet the sales amount threshold (and did not get a 1099K), if you had any sales on eBay, **you should still report this income on your taxes**. In your first year, you will not sell very much and will have expenses to deduct, so your tax liability may be small or nothing. Again, consult your local tax professional and consistently report all income.

If, after you start to get some sales on eBay, you decide that this business is for you and you want to take it further. Go ahead and register your business with your local government.

Talk to an accountant or an attorney to find out which business entity (In the US, we have LLC, Corporation, and Sole Proprietor) will be the best for you. Each entity will have its tax benefits and liabilities, and you want to ensure you take advantage of all the breaks you can get on your taxes. The more profit you get to keep, the better, but always consult with a professional before making any significant decisions.

Select a name that reflects your store inventory and personality when choosing your business name. This name will be the name your customers will associate with your store, so take some time to plan this.

Also, your local government may have free resources that you can use. Many countries have established offices to promote small businesses and may have laid out some programs you can use. They may have mentoring, free consulting, loan programs, grants, sponsorship opportunities, and more. Call around and take advantage of those.

US-Based Business Resources

If you live in the USA, here are some links to get you started:

1. Small Business Administration (SBA) - The SBA offers a variety of free resources for small business owners, including business counseling, training programs, and access to funding opportunities. https://www.sba.gov/

2. SCORE - SCORE is a nonprofit organization that provides free business mentoring and education services to entrepreneurs. They offer workshops, webinars, and one-on-one counseling sessions to help new business owners succeed. https://www.score.org/

3. Women's Business Centers (WBCs) - WBCs are a network of centers that provide training, counseling, and resources specifically for women entrepreneurs. They offer free business counseling, workshops, and access to funding opportunities. https://awbc.org/courses/

4. Small Business Development Centers (SBDCs) - SBDCs are a national network of centers that provide free one-on-one counseling, training, and resources to small business owners. They offer assistance with business planning, marketing, and accessing funding opportunities. https://americassbdc.org/

5. Veterans Business Outreach Centers (VBOCs) - VBOCs provide free resources and support to veteran entrepreneurs, including counseling, training, and access to funding opportunities. https://www.sba.gov/business-guide/grow-your-business/veteran-owned-businesses

6. Minority Business Development Agency (MBDA) - The MBDA offers a variety of free resources and support for minority entrepreneurs, including access to funding opportunities, business consulting, and training programs. https://www.mbda.gov/

7. Home Business Magazine. Packed with helpful articles and resources for the home entrepreneur. Stay updated with the latest news and articles about starting and growing your home-based business—a must-read. https://homebusinessmag.com/

8. My Own Business Institute. Take advantage of the free courses offered here. Anything from Starting a Business, creating a business plan, business insurance, and accounting. https://www.scu.edu/mobi/

9. Google. Do a simple search: "Business Startup Resources in my area," You should get results catered to where you live. Take advantage of any opportunity to learn and grow.

To find local resources in your area, a simple Google search can bring up resources you were not aware of. Take advantage of any education, funding, mentoring, manufacturing opportunities.

Networking with local business onwers can also help you expand your business by giving you access to inventory and distribution methods not available to the general public.

There are many ways to get what you need in order to be a successful business onwers, you just have to take a look and take action.

Chapter 2.
How to Get Paid on eBay

Getting paid for your sold items on eBay is one of the most important aspects of running a successful business. Cash flow is critical for any business, and eBay has made it easier than ever to get paid quickly and efficiently through Managed Payments.

Managed Payments is eBay's payment processing system that allows sellers to receive payments directly from eBay. When you enroll in Managed Payments, eBay handles all buyer payments and deposits your funds into your bank account. This means you no longer need a separate PayPal account to process payments.

This is the new (and only) way to get paid on eBay as of 2021. This is how it works:

When a buyer purchases an item from a seller enrolled in Managed Payments, the payment is processed by eBay. eBay then deducts the seller's fees and other charges, such as shipping labels, before depositing the remaining funds into the seller's bank account.

The entire process is streamlined, and the seller can view their payments, fees, and refunds in one place.

Here's how the process works step by step:

1. A buyer purchases an item from a seller on eBay

2. eBay processes the payment through Managed Payments

3. eBay deducts any fees from the payment, such as listing fees or shipping costs

4. The remaining funds are deposited directly into the seller's bank account

Your funds will be available for payout in one business day from when payment is confirmed. Once eBay clears your payout, the funds will be transferred to your bank within two business days.

For example, if the buyer pays for the item on Monday, eBay will send your payout on Wednesday to your bank. Depending on how long your bank takes to process the transfer, you will probably have access to it on Thursday or Friday.

It's important to note that sellers enrolled in Managed Payments do not have to worry about setting up payment gateways or integrating with third-party payment processors. eBay handles everything, which saves sellers time and effort.

Additionally, sellers can receive their payouts daily instead of waiting for a weekly or bi-weekly payout.

Payout schedule

eBay's default is to send your payouts daily.

As soon as your funds become available to be paid, eBay will initiate a transfer of funds two days after your buyer pays.

You can change this schedule in your Seller Hub ⇒ Payout Settings. You can change it from daily to weekly if needed.

Make sure you submit your correct bank information, so your payments are on time. The bank account needs to be a checking account. eBay currently (as of January 2021) does not accept savings or PayPal accounts for payments.

eBay will use your available funds to refund customers in case of returns or cancellations. If you do not have funds available from sales, eBay will retrieve the funds from the checking account you use for your payments.

Make sure you leave a small number of funds in your bank account. This is for refunds and cancellations that may happen in the future; you want to be prepared for those and avoid overdraft charges from your bank.

Getting paid on eBay is very easy; submit your checking account information, make sales, and receive your funds in your account.

The key is to get consistent sales, so you always have money coming in. Using the information from this book and some good hard work, you will have no problems getting deposits consistently.

Benefits of Managed Payments:

- Buyers now have more choices to pay. It's no longer required to have PayPal to shop on eBay.

Now almost all payment choices are accepted on eBay. Great for sellers!

- Sellers' reports are now in one place. Fees, refunds, payouts, returns, everything is now in one report.

- No more monthly invoices. All fees are deducted from each sale automatically. So, the payout you receive is your final profit. Store subscriptions and other options are still invoiced at the end of the month.

- Funds available can still be used to pay for shipping labels, refunds, and claims—no need to withdraw from your bank account.

If you resell full-time, opening a checking account in your business name is advisable. This will keep your personal and business income separate and can help at tax time.

Check with your local bank for requirements. They may need you to register your business with your local government authority and file tax paperwork.

Since you will probably be paying taxes on your sales at the end of the year, it's a good idea to set aside a certain amount each month so tax time will be easier and less stressful.

How to Access Managed Payments

If you need to make changes to your payment account, such as establishing or changing your checking account information. Follow these steps:

Go to your eBay page; on the top left corner, hover your mouse over your user name (Hi, username), and click "Account Settings."

On the next page, look for the "Payment" menu towards the middle of the screen. You can add or change your payment information, payout frequency, and other account preferences.

Ensure all the information is correct to ensure your payout is on time. Contact eBay directly if you have any questions or issues regarding payments.

How to Setup Managed Payments:

This payment area can be found if you look at the top left on your seller page, hover the mouse over your name, and click on "Account Settings."

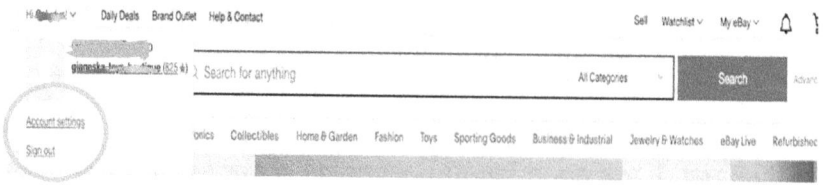

In the next section, go toward the page's middle, and click "Payments."

My eBay

Activity   Messages   **Account**

Personal Info	**Payment Information**	**Account preferences**
Business info	Payments	Permissions
Sign in and security		Advertisement Preferences
Addresses		Communication Preferences
Feedback		Close account
Request your eBay data		
Selling	**Donation Preferences**	

Enter your payment details, including your bank account information and tax identification number (if applicable). You'll also need to provide basic information about your business, such as your name and address.

Review and accept the terms: Before using managed payments, you must review and accept the terms and conditions. Please read through these carefully, as they outline your rights and responsibilities as a seller.

Set up automatic payouts: With managed payments, eBay offers the option to deposit your payouts directly into your bank account regularly. You can set up automatic payouts by going to the Payment settings section of your seller account.

Make sure you submit your correct bank information, so your payments are on time. The bank account needs to be a checking account. eBay currently (as of January 2021) does not accept savings or PayPal accounts for payments.

eBay will use your available funds to refund customers in case of returns or cancellations. If you do not have funds available from sales, eBay will retrieve the funds from the checking account you use for your payments.

Make sure you leave a small amount of money in your bank account. This is for refunds and cancellations that may happen in the future; you want to be prepared for those and avoid overdraft charges from your bank.

Start selling: Once you've completed these steps, you can start selling with managed payments! eBay will handle all payment processing and disburse your funds directly to your bank account. You can monitor your earnings and fees in your seller account, and eBay will provide regular reports and notifications to keep you up-to-date.

Benefits of Managed Payments:

- Buyers now have more choices to pay. It's no longer required to have PayPal to shop on eBay.

- Sellers' reports are now in one place. Fees, refunds, payouts, returns, everything is now in one report.

- No more monthly invoices. All fees are deducted from each sale automatically. So, the payout you receive is your final profit. Store subscriptions and other options are still invoiced at the end of the month.

- Funds available can still be used to pay for shipping labels, refunds, and claims—no need to withdraw from your bank account.

- Managed payments are flexible. You can choose daily or weekly deposits if that makes it easier for your budget.

If you resell full-time, opening a checking account in your business name is advisable. This will keep your personal and business income separate and can help at tax time.

Check with your local bank for requirements. They may need you to register your business with your local government authority and file tax paperwork.

Since you will probably be paying taxes on your sales at the end of the year, it's a good idea to set aside a certain amount each month so tax time will be easier and less stressful.

In addition to the final value fee, eBay may deduct fees for listing enhancements and your store subscription. Listing enhancements are optional features that can help your item stand out in search results, such as adding a subtitle, scheduling a listing to start at a specific time, or promoting your listing in various ways. If you choose to use these enhancements, eBay will charge a fee for each one, which will be deducted from your payout.

If you have a store subscription on eBay, you'll pay a monthly fee for access to additional features and discounts on fees. Depending on your subscription level, eBay may deduct a percentage of your sales as an additional fee. Again, these fees will be deducted automatically from your payout, and you'll be able to see a breakdown of all fees in your seller account.

Overall, eBay makes it easy to keep track of fees related to your sales. You can see a detailed breakdown of your payouts and fees in your seller account, and you'll receive regular reports and notifications to help you stay on top of your earnings.

Whether you're just starting or a seasoned seller, eBay's managed payments system offers a convenient and reliable way to get paid for your sales.

Chapter 3.
How to Research Items to Sell

You may have watched some YouTube videos about people find-ing valuable items at a thrift store, garage sale, or even acces-sible by the side of the road. You are probably wondering how they knew that thing had any value. The answer is research and experience.

This part of reselling does take some time to master. In the begin-ning, when you start to list items unless you're familiar with their value, you will need to do research. First, you need practice researching items, and second, you want to ensure an item is worth listing.

I recommend you take it slow. Learn the process right, and research items correctly to make sure they are worth your time and effort.

Once you get experience researching and selling various items, you will be much quicker to know their value. Know which keywords work best because you have sold the same thing before.

You have to look at it as trading time for money. For example, you have a vintage glass vase in your home that has been in your family for years, and you think it will sell for hundreds of dollars, so you decide to list it on eBay.

You spend an hour photographing that vase, creating the listing, creating a description, and figuring out the shipping options. When pricing the item and you finally do the research, the vase is only worth $25.

You decide to list it anyway because you already worked an hour into this, so you might as well. Then when the item sells, you spend time locating the vase, another twenty minutes finding the correct box, and packing it with enough material to protect it in transit. After eBay takes his fee, and you subtract the shipping cost and the cost of the item, you profit around $10.

You traded five hours of work for $10. That is trading time for money. That is not what being an entrepreneur is all about. You need to know your numbers and know them well, or you risk failing in any business.

If you had researched the vase before you listed it, you would have known that this vase sold for at most $25 with free shipping.

The profit needs to be there. So, you would not have listed it and wasted your time.

This is how new resellers get discouraged and quit. All that time and effort for so little profit can be very frustrating and defeating for many. I know because I have been there. I have let my excitement and enthusiasm for an item convince me that somebody will pay top dollar for it. Only to have it in my store two years later, highly discounted to take a loss, and still, nobody will buy it.

How To Research Items to Sell

With research, you want to concentrate on three things:

- Do people like what I have to sell

- How much they buy of it, and

- What is your cost to get it

Let's look at an example. Let's say you have an item in your house that you want to sell: a Fisher-Price **Little People** house.

Locate the filters on the eBay website. If you are on the computer, they are positioned on the left-hand side of the screen. On the mobile app, they are located on the right side, on top of the search results.

1. Enter in the eBay search bar, **Keywords** related to your item: Things like brand, model, type, color, size, etc.

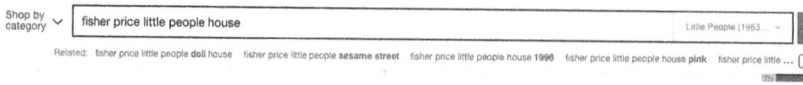

Look at the text results, and try to find your item or one that is similar.

Also, take note of the number of search results:

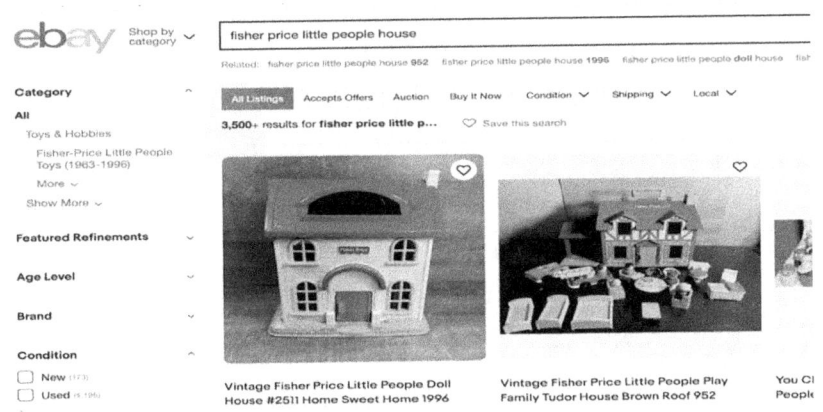

2. Since our item is used in this filter section, we select this box.

On the mobile app, the filters are located on the top right of the search results. Looking at the search results, we are still at 1300+ items available for sale, and they are all used.

This high inventory number tells us this item can be trendy and sought after. We will verify that in the next step:

3. Now, let's see how many units were actu-
   ally sold, how fast they sold, and for how much.
   Return to the filters column and select the "Sold" filter to see
   what has sold in the last 90 days. This is how long eBay will
   go back on their sold data.

As we can see below, eBay sold 992 units of this item in the last
90 days:

So, there were 1300+ available listings for this fisher price house.
Next, we saw that there were 992 SOLD listings. This means that
every 90 days, out of the 1300+ listings available, 992 get sold, or
76%. This is the item's Sales Through Rate (STR).

The Sales Through Rate (STR) is a critical metric that measures
the percentage of items that sell out of the total number of items
listed. This is the percentage of things sold in a given period, in
this case, 90 days.

Calculating your sale-through rate is straightforward. Divide the
number of listings sold by the number of available listings, then
multiply the result by 100 to express it as a percentage.

Here's the formula:

Sale-through rate = (Number of listings sold / Number of available
listings) x 100

For example, if you have 20 items listed on eBay and 10 of them sell, your sale-through rate would be:

Sale-through rate = (10 / 20) x 100 = 50%

This means that half of your listings sold, which is a good indication that your pricing and listing strategies are working well.

One way to do this calculation very quickly, especially when sourcing for inventory, is to divide the number of items sold by the total number of listings, then move the decimal point two places to the right to convert it to a percentage.

For example, if the item sold 8 out of 20 listings, you would have a sale-through rate of approximately 40%:

8 / 20 = 0.4
0.4 x 100 = 40%
(Sorry! There is math involved!)

In our Fisher Price Little People House example, 76 percent of the Little People Houses that are put up for sale get sold. This is a great STR and, therefore, a great item to sell. You will probably sell yours (given that it is in good condition and is a desirable model) in a few weeks (or earlier).

You want to keep this STR above 60% when sourcing for items. This is the best way to avoid accumulating inventory that will take a long time to sell. Remember, **you are in the reselling business, not the storage business**.

Chapter 4.

So, what are you going to sell?

This is a general question among new sellers and a very valid one. The answer is that you will need to figure out what to sell at the beginning. Clothing? Glassware? Antiques? Jewelry? Shoes? So many options and so many categories. It's easy to get overwhelmed.

I recommend starting with two or three categories you are familiar with and branching out from there.

At first, you should only go out and spend money buying inventory after some planning. Better use that money to purchase the supplies needed to start this business: tape, labels, bubble wrap, etc.

Start with items around your house. We all have stuff accumulated throughout the years that are of some value. Most items sold on eBay are in the $20 - $40 range.

Avoid heavy and expensive collectibles when you start until you become more experienced with shipping items, as these can become costly mistakes.

Start with your closet. We all are guilty of hoarding clothing items we are realistically never going to wear. Shoes that are outdated or do not fit our lifestyle anymore. Please get rid of it.

After all, these first sales are just for you to learn the eBay platform by going through actual sales. They don't have to be fancy or designer brands. They must be in good condition, with no broken or dirty parts.

Those first few sales are going to establish you as a reseller. Do a good job cleaning and preparing the item for sale (think, would I buy it?).

Take good photos, and describe them well. When it sells, pack it carefully and gracefully. Ship on time and thank the customer with feedback.

The goal at the beginning is not to make a profit but to learn by doing. Do not fall into Analysis Paralysis*. This "describes an individual or group process when overanalyzing or overthinking a situation can cause forward motion or decision-making to become "paralyzed," meaning that no solution or course of action is decided upon."

In other words, you absorb so much information that you become paralyzed or unable to take action. You have to be able to take action in this business. It's listing, shipping, sourcing, and repeat. Keep reading this book, and start looking for items to sell. You have to get started.

The following categories should get you started. Use the work-sheet on the next page and start coming up with some ideas of things to sell. Depending on where you live, you will have different sourcing opportunities. *Wikipedia contributors. (2021, February 21). Analysis paralysis. Wikipedia. https://en.wikipedia.org/wiki/Analysis_paralysis

BOLOS (Be on The Lookout)

Item Name	Notes
Ex: Nike Sneakers	Goodwill, Garage Sales, Closet

Most popular categories to sell in:

Home & Garden

Think of items that are expensive to buy new—vacuum cleaners, steamers, carpet cleaners, electrical tools, gardening machines, etc. Thrift stores and pawn shops carry these items. You can also search your local sales ads in the newspaper or online for people selling their used stuff.

You need to make sure they work before you list them. Also, make sure you weigh them in the packaging you intend to ship them in; that way, you can estimate the shipping charges.

Look in the clearance section of your local home and garden stores; they usually discount items heavily to eliminate them. Look them up on eBay. Check out the Sold listings and see if you can make a profit.

Health & Beauty

With their long shelf life and usually high retail prices, high-quality beauty, and cosmetic products are highly sought after in the resale marketplace. The biggest one is eBay.

If you spend some time browsing the SOLD listings on the eBay website, you will notice specific trends in the type of products that sell the most. High-end makeup, fragrances, perfumes, high-end skincare, and hair styling products like expensive hair dryers, straighteners, curlers, and more.

Look for known brands like Saint Laurent, Revlon, Remington, Chanel, and other medium to high-priced brands.

Vintage perfumes are big sellers. Look for them in Estate Sales, Thrift Stores, and Garage Sales.

Even if the bottle is incomplete or empty, vintage fragrances can score big bucks if you find the right ones. When you find what you think is a vintage perfume, look it up on eBay.

Remember to check the sold listings by entering the brand and fragrance name. You will be surprised at how much an old perfume bottle can get you, even with a few drops left.

Discontinued Makeup

These items can also fetch a hefty profit. Look for these in discount stores that sell liquidation merchandise. If you live in the USA, stores like TJMaxx, Marshalls, Ross, and others carry makeup and skincare items that high-end department stores have discontinued.

You can score designer hair care, high-end makeup, and perfumes in these stores at heavily discounted prices. Always look at expiration dates and the condition of packaging before you purchase.

Research the items to see how much they are being sold for on eBay. You will be surprised you can get a lot for these items no longer sold at regular stores. These are heavily sought after by loyal customers who have grown accustomed to using a product only to have the manufacturer discontinue it.

If you want to sell makeup on a grand scale, look for a local wholesale supplier to give you competitive pricing. You need to be below retail value to make any profit.

Vintage Hair Care Appliances

Hair Curlers and Rollers are enormous.

Look for the ceramic-coated ones, and make sure they have all the pieces and clips needed.

As with all products you sell, make sure to clean and sanitize these items, as well as thoroughly test them.

Look for brands like Conair, Revlon, and Remington. Look up the unit's model number on eBay, search the sold, and see how much they sell for and how often.

I have found Curler Rollers for $4 and have sold them for over $60 and more! Please research before bringing it home; some are more valuable than others.

Computers, Tablets, and Laptops

We live in a world connected by wires and computers. Always looking for the latest or just something cheap to start, people are always looking for these items. iPads have been one of the best-selling products of all time.

Look for these items in Pawn Shops, Thrift Stores, State Sales, and local marketplaces.

Vintage electronics is a category worth looking into. If you enjoy tinkering with electronics, learning and finding unique items that can bring big profits is one great way to niche your store and specialize.

Millions of collectors of vintage typewriters, radios, VCR units, DVD players, portable devices, and much more exist.

Always research before spending money on something; just because it's old does not mean it's worth anything.

Pull up your eBay app in the store and do some basic research. Locate the brand and model, input it into the eBay search, and see what you get. Look up the SOLD listings to see how many have sold and for how much.

Take note of the condition of your item compared to what's been sold. Also, try to test the equipment in the store when possible. Asking the staff can help locate remotes, cables, and a place to plug them in and test them.

If you cannot test it, check on the return policy and see if you can bring it back if it doesn't work. If the item has a very high resale value (over $100), and your cost is way cheap, sometimes it's worth taking a risk and taking it home. If it doesn't work, you can always sell it for parts.

Cell Phones

This category has exploded in recent years. There is always a new phone coming out, new technology, and new people buying and owning cell phones than ever before.

This means that people are selling their old phones on eBay for cheap, so you can take advantage and buy those phones and resell them back on eBay for a healthy profit. Many cannot afford the new phones, so they buy the latest model and buy them used on the platform. You have to learn how to test, clean, and do minor repairs like screen and battery replacement.

If you take the time to study this market and the products, you can make a very healthy profit just by flipping phones on eBay.

There is tons of information about how to do this; make sure you learn from a reputable source. However, if you are already experienced with cell phones, can keep up with current prices, and know how to repair them yourself (or where to outsource it), this can be the business for you.

Consumer Electronics

Things like headphones, speakers, and media streamers like Google Dock, Roku, and Alexa devices are trendy.

As the working-at-home revolution keeps growing, there is a tremendous demand for items to make life easier for working people.

Headphones are a big winner, as well as lamps, desks, chairs, printers, scanners, paper shredders, monitors, monitor brackets, back massagers, foot massagers, etc.

Think outside the box and beat your competition to the market. The key here is to find a reliable source to get these items at wholesale prices.

Contact distributors in your area and see if they will sell to you; many will require you to be a registered company, so check their requirements.

Clothing, Shoes & Accessories

This one is huge. As many retail stores continue closing, many have bought clothing online. The competition is fierce; there is much clothing available, and the barrier to entry is low. However, the key is always to stand out from the competition.

Look around what's available in your area. If you live close to an outlet center for big brands like Nike, Victoria's Secret, Levi's, and such, you can score many good deals on brand-new items that you can resell on eBay for many times what you paid.

The thrift stores in your area are filled with incredible vintage unique clothing items, like coats and jackets.

Pro Tip: People spend more money on a used coat than other clothing items. Because this one needs to stand the elements, and it needs to last. People tend to invest in the best coat they can afford. Always look up coats in your local thrift stores.

Sneakers are always big sellers, Nike being the winner always. However, not all Nikes are created equal. To research any Nike or sneaker shoe, look for the tag inside the shoe. The model number is usually a string of numbers, letters, or combinations.

If you want to get more into the clothing niche, your best bet is to specialize in a few categories. If they can be related, it is ideal.

For example, athletic wear is enormous and very popular. You can specialize in this and sell various items like gym gear, yoga clothing, exercise equipment, sneakers, sports equipment, and even dietary supplements and food.

Buyers into fitness and nutrition will save your store as their One Stop Shop. Repeat business is the best business.

Toys and Video Games

This category sells year around, not just during Christmas. Whether you are selling the hottest new toy or the sought-after vintage video game. People always look for toys for their kids, gifts, and collecting.

Video game console sales have exploded after the pandemic. More people are staying at home and not going out.

Parents must find a way to entertain kids indoors, and video games are one of them.

When you are out buying inventory, ensure you get as complete a set as possible. For example, if you find a console, check for controllers, cables, memory cards, adaptors, and games for it.

Try to test it in the store if you can. Ask the staff where they have a plug you can use, and they can be accommodating many times. Ensure you get the unit to power on and the disk drives open and close as they should. Look for broken and missing parts, water damage, fire damage, and overall unit wear. Don't forget to ask for the return policy.

Quickly research the eBay app and see how much they are selling for. Ensure you buy the item at 50% or lower than the ongoing reselling price.

When selling used video games and consoles, make sure you take the weight and dimensions into consideration when you are listing. If not done correctly, the shipping cost can and will eat your profit when you sell it.

Craft and Hobbies

This category has also enjoyed tremendous growth recently. With more people working from home and having more spare time, more people are getting into hobbies and collecting.

Think craft supplies like threads, yarn, needles, patterns, storage, books, and courses.

Many people have also taken to collecting. Trying to revive their hobbies, they look for vintage figurines, die-cast vehicles, puzzles, board games, and more.

Whenever you find a craft item or collectible, look it up and see its value. There is also a big market for supplies for hobbies such as knitting, sewing, jewelry making, woodworking, and more.

Books, Movies, CDs, and DVDs

This area is one of the easiest to get into, as these are abundant in places like Thrift Stores and Garage Sales. Look for brand-new sealed media and books; these tend to be the most valuable. Also, look for vintage compilations and cult classics.

Soundtracks are also a great winner in this category, especially if the movie has won awards like the Oscars or is a popular musical like Hamilton.

As with anything, research, as not all titles are valuable. If you find a large stack of movies or CDs for a very low price, and you don't have time to scan each one and research.

If you buy and, after your research, you find them to need to be more valuable when sold individually, you can always make bundles of 5 or 10 CDs and list them on eBay. You can earn back your investment and even make a few bucks. Take these experiences as learning experiences.

A collection of books (or sets) can be valuable in this category. For example, single Harry Potter books do not sell for very much, but once you have a complete set, you can make your investment many times. It pays to wait until you have all the books to create your listing of a particular series.

Seasonal Items

Whether Christmas, Saint Valentine, St. Patrick's Day, or any other holiday, eBay is a great place to buy and sell everything seasonal.

The strategy with seasonal items is straightforward: buy holiday items after the holiday has passed. The day after Christmas,

Halloween, or even new year's, many retail stores discount this holiday merchandise up to 90% off and more.

Anything from Winter gear and boots to Christmas trees, ornaments, lights, decorations, gifts, etc. You can score much inventory for pennies on the dollar on the days after Christmas.

Some people will say to wait until the seasons to start listing, but eBay is a global marketplace. It can be scorching hot where you are, but somebody somewhere will need that winter coat, those boots, and even those Christmas decorations any time of the year.

I live in the South of the United States, where it is warm all year. In my eBay store, at any given moment, I can be shipping beach board shorts, winter boots, a Christmas nativity set, and replacement pieces for a vintage Monopoly game.

It's about having the correct items and prices and composing the best listing. Have great photos and describe your item well.

Chapter 5.
How to take Photos that Sell

Regarding online sales, good-quality photos are potential buyers' first impression of your item. In a physical store, buyers can inspect the article, feel its texture, and examine it from all angles.

In the online world, buyers rely solely on product photos to make purchasing decisions. This means that taking high-quality product photos is essential for getting a potential buyer's attention and critical in building trust with the buyer.

By providing clear, detailed photos, you can give buyers a sense of the item's quality, condition, and unique features. You can bring the item to their eyes by getting close and showing those special features the buyer needs to see. Doing this will lead you to more successful sales.

Buyers will be more attracted to your pictures than anything else on your listing. They will often skip the description and buy solely based on your photographs. So, work on getting this area of your business right; this book chapter will show you how.

Get Your Lighting Right

When it comes to photographing items for online sales, lighting is vital. The proper lighting can help highlight the details of your item and make it look more appealing to potential buyers. In this article, we'll explore how to use different types of lighting to get the best results when photographing items for sale online.

Natural light

Natural light is often the best choice when photographing items to sell online. It's free, usually readily available, and can produce stunning results.

Here are a few tips for using natural light:

- Find the right spot. Look for a location near a window or outside where natural light will illuminate the item. Direct sunlight can create harsh shadows and make your photo appear dark. So, try to find a bright area that could be sunnier.

- Use a reflector. If you photograph an item with dark or shadowed areas, use a mirror to bounce light back onto those areas. A simple white piece of paper can work as a makeshift reflector. They can be very inexpensive; buy one used on eBay.

- Time of day matters. The quality and color of natural light can change during the day, so experiment with different times to find the best light for your item. Early morning and late afternoon light is often softer and more favorable for your items.

Artificial light

If natural light is not an option, or you want more control over the lighting, artificial lights can be a great choice. Here are a few kinds of artificial light to review:

Soft box lighting. Soft box lighting is artificial lighting that produces smooth, diffused light ideal for photographing items.

Softbox lights are available in various sizes and can be positioned to create the perfect lighting setup for your article. Picture of a sample softbox setup.

Ring lights. Ring lights are a type of light that surrounds the camera lens, producing even lighting on your subject. They're great for macro shots or for creating a spotlight effect on your item.

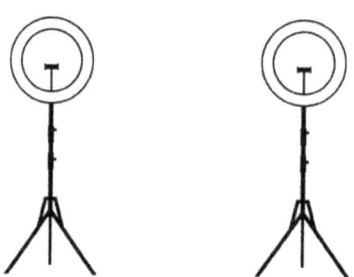

Sometimes, a couple of perfect ring lights are all you need; they are inexpensive and easy to use.

Studio lighting kits. A studio lighting kit can be an excellent investment if you're serious about photographing items for online sales. These kits come with multiple lights, stands, and diffusers to help you create the perfect lighting setup for your article.

Search on Amazon for the latest lighting kits; they come in all sizes and can be an excellent investment for your eBay business. Read the reviews and pick a size that you can grow into.

When photographing items to sell online, the proper lighting can make all the difference. It would be best to experiment with natural and artificial lights to find the perfect setup to showcase your item and attract potential buyers.

Remember to pay attention to the details, such as using a reflector or adjusting the time of day, to get the best possible results. With the proper lighting, your photos will stand out and help your item sell quickly and at the best price.

Make The Photo Area Free of Distractions

Before you stage your items, ensure that your surface is clean and free of distractions. This can be as simple as wiping down a table or using a plain white sheet as a backdrop. Remember that the cleaner the surface, the better your item will stand out in the photo.

Find a clean, neutral background that won't detract from the item. A solid-colored wall or a plain tablecloth can work well. The only items on the photos should be the item you are selling, nothing else. Unless they are essential to the listing, like a foam head for a wig, or a hanger on a dress, your item should be the center of attention.

One time I had this doll for sale, and I had her on a metal stand to stand upright. This made the doll more attractive, and it was easier to photograph all angles with the doll standing up.

However, when the doll sold, and I shipped only the doll (not the stand because it was not included), the buyer was upset and left me negative feedback. Luckily, eBay could remove it because I stated in the description that the stand was not included. Buyers rarely read descriptions and always assume based on the pictures alone.

Always specify what is included and what is not. My advice is to not photograph anything extra with your item that can create an expectation on the buyer. This will lead to returns and negative feedback.

Get Close and Personal

When taking pictures of items, get as close as possible without distorting the image. Do not take photos from far away or from high above. Potential buyers will have difficulty getting to the item's details if it's not from close.

Buyers want to get up close and personal and look at textures, fit, buttons, flaws, condition, colors, patterns, etc. They want to ensure that what they're getting is in good condition, show every angle you can, and get up close. Use all 12 picture slots in your listing; the eBay algorithm will love you for it.

Avoid Shaking The Camera

When you have many items to go through, it's easy to want to do it fast. However, avoid shaking the camera while taking pictures, or they will appear blurry.

I have spent hours photographing hundreds of items, only to notice that my pictures look blurry after I am done. Now they need to be retaken, and much time was wasted.

Carefully review each item, holding the camera steady and ensuring the pictures appear correct. Use a tripod if it helps, or rests the camera on a flat surface.

Stage The Item for Better Presentation

If you are selling clothing, don't just throw the item on the kitchen floor and expect to get top dollar for it. Would you buy clothing off somebody's floor? Not many would.

When taking photos of your item, capture it from different angles. This will give potential buyers a better sense of the object's appearance and how it might look in person. If you're selling clothing or accessories, consider taking photos of the item worn or styled differently.

Set up your camera to a high resolution. You want your photos to appear clear and not stretched. High resolution will create a higher-quality picture and a better customer experience.

Different angles and lighting can produce different colors in your pictures. Make sure what comes out in the photographs represents the item. You want the colors to be correct and the details to be right. You want to avoid returns because you describe something as black, and the item is blue.

Once you've taken your photos, don't be afraid to edit them to make them look their best. This could include cropping the photo to remove distractions, adjusting the lighting or color balance, or sharpening the image to make it look more professional.

However, be careful not to over-edit your photos, which can make them look unrealistic or artificial.

Give your potential buyers all the reasons to click on your listing and purchase.

Uploading Your Pictures to eBay

When creating eBay listings, pictures can make all the difference. High-quality photos can help your items stand out in search results and give potential buyers a better idea of what they're getting.

There are a few different ways you can upload pictures to eBay. Here are some of the most common options:

1. Use the eBay app: If you're using it on your mobile device, you can take photos directly within the app and upload them to your listing. This is a convenient option if you can't access a computer or camera.

2. Use a digital camera: If you have a digital camera, you can take photos of your items and transfer them to your computer. You can upload them to your eBay listing using the eBay website.

3. Use a scanner: If you're selling smaller items, like trading cards or stamps, you can use a scanner to create high-quality images. Just place the item on the scanner bed and scan it at a high resolution. Then, save the image to your computer and upload it to your eBay listing.

4. Photo backup services: Many sellers use cloud-based photo back-ups services like Dropbox or Google Drive to store their images. This provides an extra backup for your images and allows you to access your photos from any device easily.

5. Mac Image Drop: If you're using a Mac computer, you can use the Mac Image Drop tool to upload images to your eBay listings quickly. This tool allows you to drag and drop photos onto the eBay website.

6. eBay's Picture Manager: eBay also offers a tool allow-
    ing sellers to upload and manage their eBay listing pho-
    tos. This tool includes features like image cropping and
    resizing, and it also allows you to add watermarks to
    your photos to protect your images from theft.

Chapter 6.
How to List Items on eBay

Whether you're just starting or have been selling on eBay for a while, perfecting your listings can make all the difference in attracting buyers and making sales.

At its core, eBay is an online marketplace that allows buyers and sellers to connect and transact. As a seller, your job is to create a listing that showcases your item and provides potential buyers with all the information they need to make an informed decision.

This includes high-quality photos, detailed descriptions, accurate pricing, and relevant shipping information.

Getting your eBay listings right is crucial for a few reasons.

First and foremost, it can directly impact your sales. A well-written and visually appealing listing will catch a buyer's attention and lead to a sale. Conversely, a poorly crafted listing can turn buyers off and leave your item languishing in obscurity.

Additionally, eBay's search algorithm considers various factors when determining which listings to display in search results. The more relevant keywords you use, and the more complete your listing is, the more likely it is to show up in front of potential buyers.

In this chapter, I'll share my top tips and strategies for creating effective eBay listings that get results. Whether you're selling clothing, electronics, collectibles, or anything in between, the principles outlined in this guide can be applied to any item.

What are Keywords?

Keywords are the words and phrases people use to search for items on eBay. The terms buyers type into the search bar for specific products or categories.

When creating effective eBay listings, keywords are crucial because they can directly impact your listing's visibility in search results.

Including relevant and specific keywords in your listing title and description increases the chances of your listing appearing in front of potential buyers. This is because eBay's search algorithm considers the relevance of the keywords used in a listing when determining which listings to display to users.

If your listing includes exact or related keywords that a buyer is searching for, your item is more likely to appear at the top of the search results.

However, it's essential to use keywords strategically and avoid keyword stuffing, which is cramming in as many keywords as possible to manipulate search results. This can harm your listing's visibility and reputation on eBay, so using keywords naturally and relevantly is important.

You can list items on eBay in two ways: start a brand new listing from scratch and build it with your item specifics. Or you can use a listing that has already sold and use those keywords for your listing.

Creating a Listing from Scratch

First, once log into your eBay page, locate the "sell" link in the top right corner. This will take you to the listing form. You will be given a blank template to create your listing with your keywords.

When creating a listing from scratch, it's important to think carefully about the words you use in your title. The title is the first thing buyers see when browsing eBay, so it's crucial to make it clear and concise.

You'll want to include relevant information about the item, such as the brand, model number, and unique features or benefits. Avoid using vague or generic terms, as these are less likely to catch a buyer's attention.

Creating a Listing from a Sold Listing

Alternatively, you can use a sold listing as a starting point for your new listing.

This can be a great way to ensure that you're using keywords that have been proven to work. Look for keywords repeated in the item's title and description, and try to incorporate these into your new listing.

Overview of how to properly list your items on eBay:

Add Title and Description

Write a clear and descriptive title for your item. This should include the brand, model, and any other relevant information. The description should detail the item's condition, features, and other essential information buyers should know.

Choose a Category

Choose the category that best matches your item. eBay has many categories, so take your time to find the most appropriate one.

Add Photos

Upload clear and high-quality photos of your item. You can add up to 12 pictures for free. Take photos from different angles to help buyers see the article in detail. Show any flaws, special features, textures, etc.

Set a Price

Set a price for your item. (See the Chapter on Pricing your Items) You can sell it for a fixed price or through an auction. You can set a starting price and duration if you choose an auction.

Set Shipping Options

Decide how you want to ship the item and how much you want to charge for shipping. You can also choose to offer free shipping. Refer to the shipping chapter for more information on this.

Payment and Returns

Set up your payment and return policies on your eBay account page. Refer to the chapter on Payments and Returns for the best practices to do this.

Review and publish.

Let's create a sample eBay listing:

Let's say you have a Michael Kors dress you have not worn in years; it's in good condition, and you want to sell it. The first thing you need to do is to come up with keywords for your item. This is how you do it:

Start with the eBay search bar and enter descriptive words (keywords) about your item. Things like brand, color, and function, and go from there. For this example (we have a dress to sell), you start with: "Michael Kors Pink Dress" as the keyword.

Also, in filters, select the "Sold" option to see the keywords used for the sold dresses.

Now let's look for a dress that is very similar to yours.

Once you find it, which keywords did they use? How did they describe it in the description? How did they take their photos? Did they get top dollar for it? That is the listing you want to model after.

Notice they use words like Sheath, Slip On, Maxi, Abstract, Sleeveless, Size Medium, Stretch, Floral, etc. Those are Keywords, search terms that people search for when looking for this type of item.

From the search results, I am going to pick this listing because it is the one that resembles my dress the most:

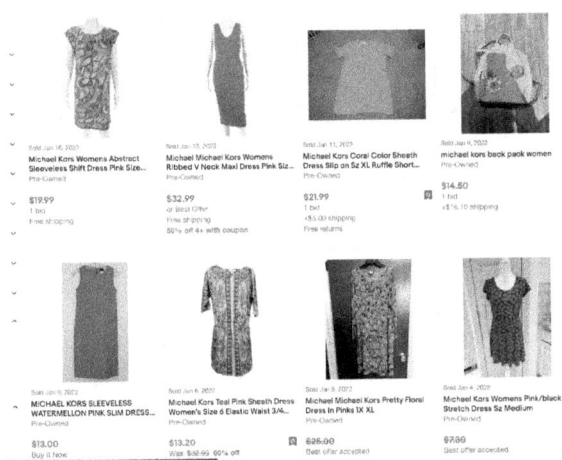

Next:

Click on the listing to open it, and you should see this:

Click on "Sell One like this," eBay opens a new page with a form to create a new listing. However, this one will have the sold item's information, including the title.

We will NOT use the same title as written because that will be wrong. We will use the main keywords that help us describe our item, but we will add the unique characteristics of OUR item to the title.

We are using this listing title as a template: "Michael Kors Black White Gathered Waist Sleeveless Scoop Neck Dress Sz. M"

We can compose this new title based on our dress: "Michael Kors Pink Yellow Belt Sleeveless V Neck Dress Size 8 Casual Work Office."

Use those keywords you found in this sold listing, and add key-words describing your specific item in your title.

As you become experienced in researching various items, com-ing up with winning keywords will become routine, and you will be able to list more quicker. That is why it is essential to niche your store and specialize in listing similar items.

If you want to be found by buyers wanting what you are selling, you must give it to them as quickly as possible. And that means using keywords in your titles that people are using to search.

Here are some tips when it comes to creating your profitable eBay title:

- Include specifics for your item—size, condition, color, flaws, special edition, etc.

- State what your item is—for example, Dress, Toaster Oven, Doll, etc. Be specific.

- Do not use words like GREAT, AMAZING, or RARE. These make your listings look amateurish and unprofessional.

- Do not include prices, either retail or your price. Only write this in the pricing area of the listing.

- Do not include commas, asterisks, emojis, symbols, exclamation points, etc. These need to be clarified for eBay's algorithm and may prevent your listing from appearing in search results.

- Make sure you correct any spelling mistakes. Do not use abbreviations; use complete words.

- Refrain from including information that can be misleading. Suggesting your item is a different (better) brand or stating the product is a "Best Seller," etc.

- Don't use all caps. It means you're screaming in text.

- Your title must sound natural and not be pushy, spammy, unprofessional, or childish.

- Try to use all 80 characters in your title.
  Longer titles are known to bring more sales; the more detail you can provide, the more clicks you will get for your items.

- Include your primary keyword (item name: Dress, Pants, Doll, etc.) at the beginning of your title.

- Reassure your buyers by including words like "Official" and "Authentic" in your titles for items where this applies (collectibles, artwork, designer brands, etc.)

- Capitalize each word in your title; it makes it easier to read.

- One great rule to follow when creating your titles is: Describe your product + Features + Item's Benefits.

For example, let's say you have a memory card to sell. Using the formula above, we can easily create a title that includes all the information a potential buyer wants.

Example of a wrong title:

"Memory card 120 GB", Why is this the wrong title?

- No indication that the item is new or used

- No brand or type necessary for compatibility with devices

- It looks like the seller made absolutely no effort.

eBay's algorithm has little information to go on. You are causing your listing to be pushed to the bottom and never seen by anyone.

Example of a good title:

- "New Samsung SD Memory Card 120 GB PC Mac Camera Free Shipping."

- Great keywords! People looking for memory cards seek these keywords to ensure they buy the right product.

- eBay's algorithm loves this; it will be shown to more potential buyers looking for new cards, 120GB specific cards, and cards they can use with their cameras.

- Standing out by offering a better value increases your chances of making a sale. People love free stuff, especially free shipping.

Compose Winning Descriptions

When selling on eBay, crafting an adequate item description is one of the most important factors for success. Your description should be thorough, accurate, and compelling, providing potential buyers with all the information they need to make an informed purchasing decision.

Here are some tips for composing descriptions that will help bring sales:

- **Use descriptive language**: Be sure to use descriptive language in your item description, and avoid using generic or vague terms. This will help potential buyers understand precisely what they are getting and what to expect when they receive the item.

- **Please include all relevant details**: When composing your item description, have all relevant information about the item, including its condition, size, color, functionality, and other essential features. This will help potential buyers understand precisely what they are getting and what to expect when they receive the item.

- **Use high-quality photos**: Along with a thorough item description, high-quality images are essential for attracting potential buyers. Take clear, well-lit photos that showcase the item from multiple angles.

- **Be honest**: Honesty is essential when it comes to selling on eBay. Be upfront about any flaws or imperfections in the item, and mention them in your item description.

- **Provide excellent customer service**: Finally, ensure excellent customer service throughout the transaction process. This includes responding promptly to buyer inquiries, shipping items, and resolving any issues that may arise during the transaction.

- **Organize your information.** Make it easy for a potential buyer to scan through your listing quickly. Separate your information into paragraphs or bullet points.

- **Be clear about what is included.** Only include items in photos that are included with your listing. If you are using props or anything else, be evident in the description about what is included and what is not.

- **Correct your grammar and spelling.** Your listings should convey a professional demeanor.

- **Include your Return Policy.** A short sentence stating whether you accept returns or not and for how long is usually customary.

  However, you don't want to fill this area with many No's and come off as negative. For example, I have seen return policies like:

"ABSOLUTELY NO RETURNS FOR ANY REASON WHATSOEVER!!!!!!"

Would you buy from this seller? I would not. She comes off as negative and somebody who will not be reasonable if I have a problem with my purchase.

Don't do this. Instead, write something like this:|

RETURN POLICY:

"30 Days return. If you are unsatisfied with your purchase, please get in touch with us, and we will make it right."

That brief statement comes off as friendly and sincere. I would feel comfortable buying from this seller. This is the positive feeling you want to invoke in your customers.

By following these tips and crafting effective item descriptions, you can help ensure that your eBay listings attract potential buyers and lead to successful sales.

Item Specifics

Adding item specifics to your eBay listing is very important for the success of your eBay store. Item specifics are details about your item, such as size, color, material, and brand, that help potential buyers find and filter your item in search results.

Here are some essential reasons why you should add item specifics to your listing:

- Boost visibility: When buyers search for items on eBay, they often use specific keywords or filters to narrow down their results. Adding accurate and detailed item specifics to your listing increases the chances of your item appearing in those filters and getting seen by potential buyers.

- Improve buyer confidence: When buyers see that you have provided detailed and accurate information about your item, they are more likely to trust you and make a purchase. Item specifics can also help prevent misunderstandings or disputes about the item's details or condition.

- Save time: By providing as many item specifics as possible in your listing, you reduce the likelihood of receiving questions from potential buyers asking for additional information. This can save you time and help streamline the selling process.

To make the most out of your item specifics, it's important to choose the most relevant and specific categories for your item. Here are some tips to keep in mind:

- Be specific: Choose the most specific category that accurately describes your item. Avoid general categories that could be applied to a wide range of items.

- Use eBay's suggestions: eBay provides suggestions for item specifics based on your chosen category. Please take advantage of these suggestions and use them whenever possible.

- Check your spelling: Make sure to spell your item specifics correctly. Misspellings can cause your item to not show up in search results.

- Be accurate: Provide accurate and truthful information about your item. Misleading information can lead to buyer disputes and negative feedback.

In addition, including item specifics in your listing can help your item appear in search results on eBay and search engines like Google. This is because eBay provides Google with structured data for its listings, which includes the item specifics.

Google then uses this information to display eBay listings in search results, making it easier for buyers to find the items they are looking for even if they are not searching on eBay directly.

Therefore, including item specifics can improve the visibility of your eBay listings and increase your chances of making a sale.

How To Choose the Right Category

When listing an item on eBay, choosing the right category is crucial to ensure that your item is visible to potential buyers. Here are some key points to keep in mind when selecting the category for your item:

Importance of Category: Selecting the right category ensures that your item is easily found by buyers who are searching for similar items. This helps increase the chances of your item selling quickly and for the best possible price.

Research your options: Before selecting a category, take some time to research your options. Look at other listings for similar items and see where they're categorized. This can help you better understand which categories are most relevant to your item.

Use eBay's Category Suggestions: eBay has a feature called Category Suggestions that can help you find the best category for your item. Enter keywords describing your item, and eBay will suggest the most relevant categories.

Consider subcategories: Some categories on eBay have subcategories that can help further refine the search results for your item. Consider selecting a subcategory if it's relevant to your item.

Be specific: Choose the most specific category possible for your item. This ensures that buyers looking for exactly what you're selling will find your listing.

Use brand names: eBay has categories named after the most famous brands. For example, if you have a Barbie doll, don't list it under "Toys > Dolls." Drill down (or search) categories and look for "Barbie."

In this example, eBay has an extensive subcategory for Barbie dolls. They include everything from Vintage, Special Editions, Exclusive releases, accessories, and more. Many buyers will go to specific categories to look for items. Help them find yours.

By taking the time to research your options and choose the most relevant category, you can ensure that potential buyers easily find your item on eBay. This can help increase your chances of a successful sale and boost your profits.

Grading your Item Condition

When it comes to selling on eBay, accurately describing the condition of your item is crucial. Not only is it essential to provide potential buyers with a clear understanding of the item they are considering, but it can also prevent any potential issues with returns or negative feedback.

Here are some options when grading the condition of your item:

- New: This refers to an item that has never been used or opened and is still in its original packaging.

- Like New: This refers to an item that has been opened but is in excellent condition with no signs of wear or damage.

- Very Good: This refers to an item that has been gently used and shows minimal signs of wear or damage.

- Good: This refers to an item that has been used and shows signs of wear or damage but is still functional.

- Fair: This refers to an item that has been heavily used and shows signs of wear or damage but is still functional.

- Poor: refers to an item in very rough condition, with significant damage or wear that may affect its functionality.

- For Parts or Repair: Items that do not work but can be used for parts to repair other units.

Never assume that an item is brand new just because it's wrapped in plastic or the packaging looks new. Always inspect if the item has been taken out of the box or used in any way. Grade your items accordingly and price accordingly.

Here are some tips for evaluating your item's condition:

- Inspect every single item carefully. Test every electrical item, even if it has the original package attached to it. Many people will donate defective items in their original boxes to the thrift store; they do this to avoid returning them to the store. It happens; that's why you must do your due diligence and inspect your items for their functionality and condition.

- Test the item's functionality. If it's a VCR, put tape on it for a while to make sure it runs. If it's a clock, put some in batteries, or plug it in. Always make sure the functions work as intended.

- Inspect all battery compartments of electrical items for corrosion. Old things are left with batteries inside for a long time (sometimes years), causing them to leak and corrode the contacts.

- Look for expiration dates. Make sure you photograph the label and indicate this in your description. Many items are sold past their expiration date with no problem.

Do your research to find out if your item is one of those. Things like ink toner and some cosmetics are perfectly fine sold and used past their expiration date. Just disclose this in your photos, title, and description.

Selling items "For Parts or Repair."

Selling items for parts or repair on eBay can be a great way to profit from items that may not be in working order. Many buyers are willing to purchase items that are not functioning if they believe they can fix them or use them for parts.

When listing items for parts or repair, it's essential to be honest and clear about the item's condition. It's a good idea to include detailed photos of any damage or parts that may be missing.

Be sure to describe the item's functionality or lack thereof as accurately as possible. This will help to avoid any misunderstandings with buyers and prevent negative feedback.

When pricing items for parts or repair, finding the right balance between making a profit and pricing the item reasonably can be challenging. It's important to research similar items on eBay to understand what they sell for in their current condition and how much they sell broken.

Another tip is to consider selling items for parts individually instead of as a whole. For example, if you have a broken phone, you may be able to sell the screen, battery, and other parts separately for a higher profit than selling the entire phone as a whole.

Finally, when selling items for parts or repair, it's important to communicate with buyers promptly and honestly. Be sure to answer any questions they may have and provide accurate information about the item's condition.

By providing excellent customer service, you can help to build a positive reputation on eBay and increase your sales.

Chapter 7

How to Ship on eBay

Shipping is a crucial part of the selling process, and understanding how to ship your items correctly can help you maximize your profits and avoid costly mistakes. In this guide, I'll share tips and strategies for shipping your eBay items quickly, safely, and cost-effectively.

One of the most significant benefits of learning how to ship items on eBay correctly is that it can help you avoid overcharges and maximize your profits.

Shipping costs can quickly eat into your margins if you're not careful, and inaccurate shipping estimates can lead to unhappy customers and negative feedback.

By learning to accurately calculate shipping costs, choose the correct shipping method, and package your items properly, you can save money on shipping and provide a positive customer experience.

In addition to saving money on shipping, learning shipping practices can help you build a reputation as a reliable and professional seller. By providing fast and reliable shipping and packaging your items securely, you can increase customer satisfaction and earn positive feedback, which can, in turn, lead to more sales.

By mastering the art of shipping on eBay, you can take your selling game to the next level and increase your profits. In this chapter, I'll provide tips and strategies for accurate shipping cost calculation, choosing the suitable shipping method, packaging your items, and more.

Shipping in the USA

NOTE: These instructions apply specifically to the USA shipping system. However, some of these concepts may apply to various shipping systems. Please check with your local postal service to get familiar with their packaging rates, rules, and regulations.

In the USA: You have two options when it comes to charging for shipping:

Flat Rate: You set the amount the buyer will pay regardless of location. Do this only when you are experienced in shipping the same package type, and know with most certainty how much the cost will be.

Calculated: The amount the buyer pays depends mainly on their location. Select this option for most packages, and your measurements and weight are correct.

How to Measure your Packages

Boxes are measured like this: L x W x H (Length x Width Height)

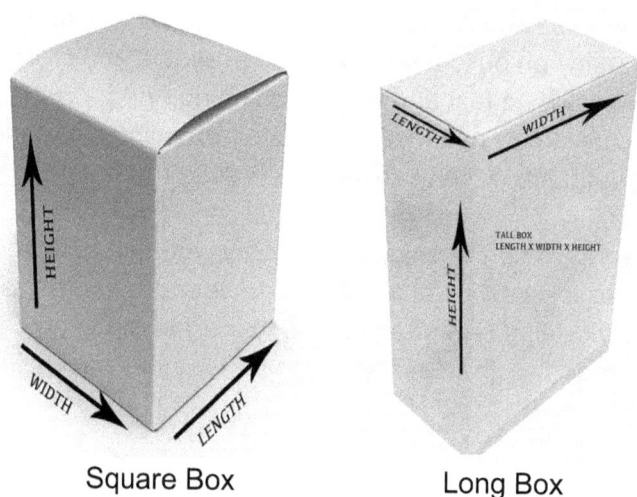

Square Box	Long Box

How to Weigh your Packages

A weight scale is one of the first things you must purchase before selling anything online. It doesn't have to be fancy or expensive; a simple $15-$20 scale from Amazon or eBay will be fine.

Make sure it is sturdy and can go up to 50 lbs. I doubt you will sell anything heavier than that. If you do, you can always upgrade later.

Make sure that when you weigh your items, the scale is flat and free from anything that may affect the weight of your item.

How to Ship with the USPS Service

This book was written mainly for those who live in the USA. Since I lack experience shipping from any other country, I cannot give any information on any other shipping system.

Even though most of these tips can be used for shipping items with any service, anywhere in the world, please consult with your local shipping service for more information on how to ship your items and how they handle international shipping and customs practices. A simple google search should connect you with your local postal agency, where you can read up on how they handle packages.

Start shipping with USPS.

When starting, the Postal Service will be the system you want to learn first. This is because most of the packages will be cheaper to ship through them than through any other carrier.

eBay has negotiated discounts with all the major shipping carriers for all their sellers. If you print your shipping label at home using eBay, this means you can save about 30% in postage versus purchasing at a Post Office counter.

Select your shipping service:

Measure your item in the packaging with the instructions above. Weight your item. If your item is 16 oz or less, you can send it "First class," the cheapest option available from the postal service.

If your item is over 16oz, you need to ship it via Priority Mail, Parcel Post, or Media Mail (Medial Mail only if you are sending books and some types of media, please refer to the USPS.com website for more information on how to ship Media Mail, and what items are allowed).

First Class Postage

This can be anything from a postcard to a pair of light shoes. You can choose this service if it weighs under 16oz and measures less than 108 inches in length and girth combined.

You can use any packaging as long as it's clean, it's free of other shipping labels, barcodes, or other information that may interfere with scanning and tracking.

Make sure you only use regular letter envelopes to ship things other than plain paper. Shipping unbendable more oversized items using a standard white envelope will jam and break the USPS machines. Please don't do it.

Delivery times vary from 3-7 days. However, I have seen this time go from one day if it's local to over ten days traveling across the country.

When shipping from home, ensure you are honest about your measurements and weight.

The USPS can and will charge you again for any overages. I have seen them only deliver a package once they are paid an additional amount. This can create a bad customer experience.

Priority Mail

If your package does not meet the First Class Package requirements, you must send it via Priority Mail. You can use your boxes and packaging or the boxes that the USPS (USA) provides for free.

USPS Free Boxes

There are two kinds of boxes you can get for free from the USPS. Flat Rate or Mailing Boxes. Let's look at each individually:

Flat Rate Priority Mail Boxes

These boxes come in various sizes and have a fixed price for shipping, regardless of the weight or destination of the package.

This means you can ship a heavy item for the same price as a lighter one, saving you money in certain situations. However, only use these boxes when they are the cheapest option; in most cases, they will not be. When preparing your shipments, always compare rates to see which is more affordable.

How to Ship with "Flat Rate" Priority Mail Boxes:

1. Choose the correct box: Select the flat rate box that is appropriate for the size and weight of your item.

2. Pack your item: Pack your item securely in the box, making sure to use plenty of packing materials to prevent damage during shipping.

3. Seal the box: Tape the box securely with shipping tape.

4. Fill out the label: Fill out the shipping label with the recipient's and your return address.

5.   Drop off at the post office: Take your package to the post office or schedule a pickup.

USPS Mailing Boxes

These boxes come in various sizes and are charged based on weight and destination. So depending on how far you are from the destination and how much your package weighs, you will be charged accordingly.

This contrast with flat rate boxes, where you are charged one fee regardless of weight and destination as long as the item fits in the box. With these boxes, the fee varies.

Here are the pros and cons of using USPS free mailing boxes:

Pros:

1.   Cost-effective: As mentioned earlier, these boxes are completely free to use, so you can save money on both the package and the shipping costs.

2.   Easy to use: Free mailing boxes are easy to use and require minimal packing materials. Pack your item in the box, tape it up, and you're ready to ship!

3.   Fast delivery: The free mailing boxes come with priority mail shipping, which means your package will be delivered within 1-3 business days.

4.   Wide range of sizes: There are a variety of box sizes to choose from, so you can find the perfect box for your item.

Cons:

1. Limited destinations: Free mailing boxes are only available for shipping within the United States, so if you need to ship internationally, you must use a different shipping method.

2. Size restrictions: Each box has a weight limit, so if your item exceeds the limit, you must use a different shipping method.

3. Limited design options: The free mailing boxes have a standard USPS design, which may only be suitable for some items.

Using free mailing boxes from USPS is a great way to save money on shipping costs, especially for smaller items. Plus, the convenience of having the packages delivered to your doorstep can be a big time-saver.

To order your free Priority boxes: go to USPS.com. Just locate the Postal Store link at the top of the page, then select Shipping Supplies. Your free order will be delivered via regular mail by your local carrier.

These take two or more weeks to receive, depending on demand—also, only order what you need now.

Once you get an idea of how many supplies you use, then order accordingly.

These are the boxes I recommend you order:

Padded Flat Rate Envelopes Priority Mail Shoe Box

Priority Mail Mailing Box - 7. This one measures 12x12x8 inches. This is one of the most versatile boxes they offer.

Priority Mail Flat Rate Boxes Variety Pack.

This is a great bundle to get so you can get familiar with the many sizes of these boxes.

For example, I ship a lot of 18-inch dolls, a couple of cuts with my scissors, and the free mailing box 12x12x8 turns into a perfect fit. Look for "Shipping Box hacks" on Google.

How to Choose a Shipping Carrier:

There are three options for choosing a carrier on eBay: USPS (United States Postal Service), FedEx, and UPS.

USPS

Some of the benefits of using USPS:

Rates for all packages under 1 pound or 16oz. They are lower than anyone else.

You can schedule a pick-up on the USPS.com website. This must be prepared the day before. The postman will pick it up during your regular mail delivery time. You can also schedule a pick-up at a specific time, but there is a fee for this.

You must create an account to order free shipping supplies on their website. See the previous section.

Once you drop off your packages and receive a receipt, eBay will be notified that you have shipped your packages. The buyer will get an email too.

FedEx

Some of the Benefits and tips using FedEx

- Great rates for heavy packages.

- You must use clean boxes and tape them well. FedEx is very picky about which packages they accept.

- Drop-off locations are conveniently located in local stores near you. Check their website for drop-off locations.

- Packages dropped off and scanned trigger a notification from eBay to the buyer.

- Usually faster than USPS.

- A pickup service is available with some accounts.

UPS

- Same benefits as FedEx:

- If you have an account with them, you can arrange a pick-up from your location and get free labels and tracking.

- Usually faster than USPS.

- Drop-off locations are conveniently located in local stores near you. Check their website for drop-off locations.

How To Estimate Your Shipping Charges

You must estimate your shipping charges correctly when you sell items on eBay. If you do, you could save money on shipping or charge your customers less.

Here are some ways to estimate your shipping charges:

1. Use the eBay shipping calculator: eBay provides a shipping calculator that you can use to estimate your shipping costs.

2. To use it, enter the weight and dimensions of your package and the destination zip code.

3. The calculator will provide you with shipping options and their associated costs.

    A good tip is to use a zip code on the opposite side of the country. For example, in South Florida, you can use the zip code 90210 in California. This will give you the best-case scenario for your estimation of shipping charges.

4. Check with your preferred carrier: If you have a preferred carrier, such as USPS, FedEx, or UPS, you can check their website for shipping rates. They usually provide a shipping calculator as well, giving you an idea of how much you should charge for shipping.

5. Use a third-party shipping calculator: Several third-party shipping calculators are available online, such as PirateShip.com. These calculators can help you compare shipping rates across different carriers and find the best option.

6. Consider packaging materials: Remember to factor in the cost of packaging materials, such as boxes, tape, and packing peanuts. These costs can add up quickly, so include them in your shipping estimate.

Here are some helpful links to resources that can help you estimate your shipping charges:

- eBay shipping calculator: **https://www.ebay.com/shp/Calculator**

- USPS shipping calculator: **https://postcalc.usps.com/**

- FedEx shipping calculator: **https://www.fedex.com/en-us/shipping/rates.html**

- UPS shipping calculator: **https://www.ups.com/us/en/shipping/services/domestic/ground.page**

Remember, estimating your shipping charges accurately is essential, so you don't lose money or overcharge your customers. By using the resources available to you and factoring in the cost of packaging materials, you can ensure you get the correct shipping price for your items.

How to ship Internationally with eBay

eBay makes it easy for you to offer your items to millions of buyers worldwide. They do this with the Global Shipping Program. You must be enrolled in this program before using it in your listings. This is how you do it (As of this printing, January 2021):

Locate your shipping preferences by going to your "Account Settings." They are under your name, on the top left corner of your eBay page.

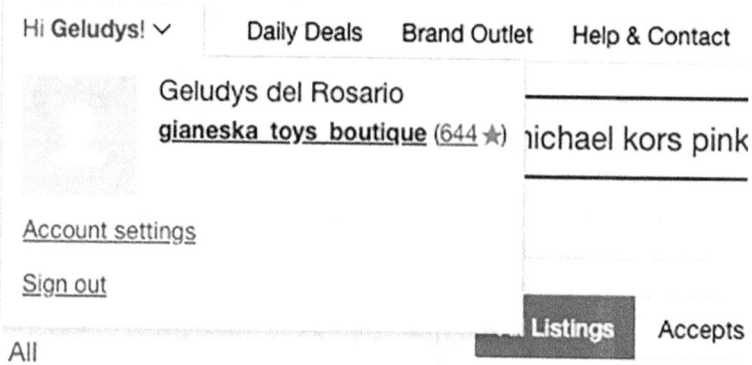

Next, on the right side of the screen, under "Account," select "Shipping Preferences."

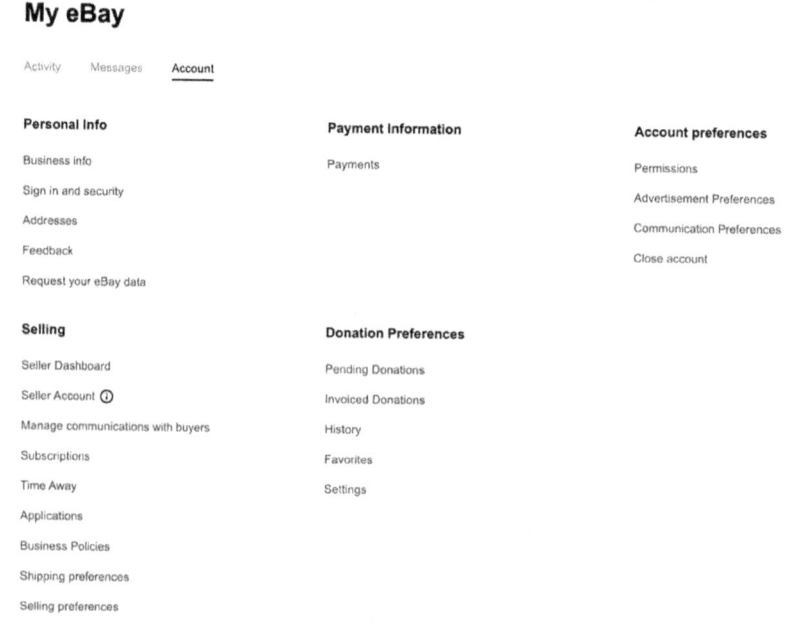

On the next screen, locate "Global Shipping Program" right on top of the page. Click on "Edit" and enroll. And that's it! Your listings will be shared with the world.

Shipping Preferences

Shipping service	Status	Actions
eBay International Shipping (NEW)	Enrolled	Opt out

Simply ship the item to our domestic shipping hub and we'll handle the rest - at no extra cost to you. **More details**

On this page, you can also set up some other options. You can exclude locations you don't want to ship to. You can establish some shipping rules for bundling items and combined payments. These are relatively advanced options, so until you are more familiar with them, leave them as they are.

So now, when listing items, select "Ship Internationally through the Global Shipping Program" once you get to the shipping section. That's it.

So what happens when you sell an item to an international buyer?

Suppose a buyer in France buys your item, and you are in California. On the order page, you may notice that there will be two addresses, but only one will print on your shipping label. The address will likely be located in Kentucky. This is where the Global Shipping center for eBay resides, and all international shipments get sent.

Once your item arrives at this center, eBay's staff will prepare all the necessary customs paperwork and ship it to the destination country.

Sometimes they will repackage the item to make it safer for traveling and open it for inspection. The package is then handed to the destination country's mailing service and delivered to the buyer.

Your responsibility ends once the package is delivered to the shipping center in the USA. Once it's sent internationally, the best you can do is track it through the sales order on your eBay page. It can take anywhere from a few weeks to a few months, depending on where it's going.

Keep in touch with your buyer to ensure they are informed of the process and know that you give them to service after the sale. If there is a problem with the delivery or damage to the item, contact eBay immediately.

Ask the buyer to send you photos of the damage and any other information they may have. Forward all to eBay for investigation. I only had one incident where the item was damaged during international delivery, and eBay quickly refunded the buyer and myself.

Buyers outside the USA will pay good money for the item they want. The service is not cheap, but it offers them an option to buy goods they can't get where they live.

How to Save 50% Or More On Your Shipping Costs

Pirateship.com* will let you take advantage of cubic rate shipping if you are in the USA. These low rates are reserved for high-volume sellers shipping 50,000 packages yearly. Pirate Ship will let you tap into these great low rates for your packages for free; you only have to buy your postage from their site.

Benefits of Using Pirate Ship:

- Pirate ship is free to use. All you need is to sign up for a free account, enter your payment information, and you are ready to ship using the lowest rates you can get.

- Access to Cubic Rate Shipping. These are calculated by size, not weight. You are to measure your packages using this formula: Length x Width x Height.

  If your package is over 18 inches tall, it does not qualify for cubic rate shipping.

- Pirate ship integrates with eBay.

  You can connect your eBay store and download your orders directly from their website into the Pirate Ship interface.

- From their website, you can enter your dimensions and weight, generate your rate, pay for your postage with a button, and print your label. It's that easy.

The first month I used them, I saw my shipping cost decrease by 35%. The following month, I cut my shipping cost even more because most packages qualify for cubic rates.

The honesty rule applies here as well. The carrier and Pirate Ship will charge your account any overages resulting in the package's weight or size being different than what the label says. Please don't do it.

*The author is not associated with PirateShip.com in any way. Nor does she receive any payment to mention this company.

Here Are Some Tips When Shipping Your eBay Items:

Getting shipping wrong is the easiest way to feel encouraged and fail in this business. Don't let it happen to you. Spend some time, in the beginning, improving your shipping process and becoming more efficient. As you become more experienced, establish a system that works for you and improves over time.

- Always ship on time. If you promise next-day shipping on your listings, then that is what your customer expects. "Under promise, over deliver" applies here as well.

eBay will track how late (or early) you ship your sales. They use the date stamp when the shipping carrier scans your packages. If you start to have a high shipping default rate, eBay will consider your account to be of "Poor Performance," which may limit your items' visibility to potential buyers. So ship on time, and avoid being pushed to the bottom.

- Insurance is necessary for valuable items or those valued at over $100 and fragile collectibles that can break in transit.

Insurance is inexpensive and can become handy should the package be damaged or lost. If you choose Priority Mail for your package, the insurance is included for up to $100. If you need more coverage, you can purchase it when you purchase your label through eBay or Pirate Ship.

Avoid negative feedback about inadequate packaging that resulted in damage. Always pack your packages with clean supplies and make sure they are secured.

- If you are starting eBay, spend only a little on shipping supplies. Finding free supplies is easy if you take the time and effort to look.

Look for furniture, big box, and auto part stores locally in your community. Many of these items are shipped to them in bubble wrap, packing bags, and packages that you can use. Call them and see if they'll give it to you for free.

Always ask permission before you take anything, and be aware of local laws if you go into a public dumpster.

- If you decide to buy supplies, buy from some fellow eBay seller on the website. Many sellers offer deals on every-thing from plastic mailers to bubble wrap and boxes. You will find many deals on eBay.com, and you will be sup-porting a small business.

- If you need help getting to the post office regularly. Take advantage of the free pick-up service by your local postal service.

- Take care of your postman. They work hard and are under an extreme amount of pressure daily. A small bas-ket with water bottles and snacks on your porch does not hurt.

My mail lady has told me many times that there are days when she can't even stop for lunch. She starts at 8 am and doesn't stop until 7 PM or later daily. I ensure she gets a Christmas card every year with some cash and words of appreciation.

Relationships are everything in this business. From the thrift store cashier to the manager. To the mail lady or UPS guy who comes daily to pick up your packages. Take care of your team.

Shipping Troubleshooting

As your eBay store grows and you start to get more and more sales, you will need help to keep track of every package.

If the item has stopped tracking for several days (or weeks), here is what I recommend you do:

Get in touch with the customer and acknowledge their request. Respond that you are contacting your post office and the buyer's post office and looking into it.

Google "USPS find missing mail." File a claim for missing mail on the USPS website.

Wait a couple of days before contacting USPS by phone. In my experience, 95% of packages I initiate a claim on start tracking are delivered within a few days.

If more than a week has passed and still no tracking or notification. Contact USPS by phone at 1- 800-275-8777, and explain your issue. Many times, they will be able to contact the local headmaster and expedite your claim.

Plan on being patient; getting an agent on the phone can take a while.

If tracking on the item says delivered, your buyer claims he did not receive it.

Once the carrier marks this item as delivered, your responsibility ends there. This is an issue to take on with the carrier of the package. Your buyer needs to go to his local post office and find out what happened during delivery.

It is good customer service to help this customer with this issue, even though it's technically out of your hands once the package has been marked delivered.

Here is what you should advise your customer to do:

Instruct your buyer to wait until the next day after tracking shows delivered. Some carriers scan packages as "Delivered" before leaving their facility.

Some carriers mistakenly scan packages as delivered and are still in the delivery truck until the next day. This happens when the carrier runs out of time that day or has no safe place to leave the package.

If the package still does not show up the next day, the buyer needs to contact their local post office and find out who the delivery person was and what happened on that route.

Ask to speak to a manager and tell them about the package. Usually, they can tell you if the carrier still has the parcel and when it will be delivered.

Ask the buyer to do a quick search outside their house. Delivery drivers are usually in a hurry and will try to conceal the packages with floor mats, bushes, chairs, doors, or anything they can find to keep your package from being stolen. Look around outside.

Ask neighbors. Chances are the carrier delivered the package to the wrong mailbox or porch. Ask around to see if anyone has received your package.

Unfortunately, as you go through selling online, you will start to notice when people are being honest and not. However, there is no sure way to tell. Sometimes we have to remind them that it is not very ethical and does have consequences.

Sometimes you get a customer who will try to get a free item (scam to get the item for free). They will lie and say that the package was never received when in fact, it was. Here is a message that I send to them when they insist the package is lost (and tracking shows delivered). If they are being dishonest, this can do the trick:

"I acknowledge your request that you have not received your item; however, as tracking shows, the Postal Service received my package, which shows it delivered on (DATE). As a courtesy

to you, I will contact your local post office and speak with the postmaster.

This will have to be investigated why the tracking shows delivered when it was not. Your local delivery person must be questioned to determine precisely what happened to your package."

If somebody lies, they will not want this investigation to go forward. Messing with the mail and the Postal Service is a criminal offense.

It has been my experience that after I send the above note, the package either magically appears or I don't hear from them again.

Of course, every case is different; always try to work with the buyer to find their package and be courteous and professional.

When To File for Insurance

As an eBay seller, one of the biggest concerns when shipping your items is the possibility of damage or loss during transit. Fortunately, most shipping carriers offer insurance that can help cover the cost of any damage or loss.

Here are some key points to keep in mind when considering filing an insurance claim:

- When to file: If an item is damaged or lost during transit, you should immediately file a claim with the shipping carrier. Most carriers have a time limit for filing claims, so acting quickly is essential.

- Reasons to file: You may want to file a claim for insurance if an item arrives damaged or doesn't arrive. It's important to have evidence of the item's condition before it was shipped, such as photos or video, to support your claim.

- How to file: To file a claim, you'll need to provide the carrier with specific information about the shipment, including the tracking number, date of shipment, and a description of the item. You may also need to provide evidence of the item's value, such as a receipt or invoice.

- Tips for success: Package your items carefully and securely to increase your chances of a successful insurance claim. Please take photos or videos of the item before it is shipped, and keep all documentation related to the sale and shipment of the item.

Filing an insurance claim can be lengthy and sometimes frustrating, but protecting yourself and your business is important.

Take the time to understand the requirements of the carrier and follow their guidelines for filing a claim. Doing so can ensure you're reimbursed for any damage or loss during transit.

Chapter 8.
How Price Your Items

When it comes to selling items on eBay, pricing is one of the most crucial factors that can determine the success or failure of your sale. You want to ensure your item is priced competitively enough to attract potential buyers while maximizing profits.

In this chapter, we'll cover how to price your item to sell on eBay based on what has sold and what's available.

Step-by-Step Guide to Price Your Items:

Step 1: Research what has been sold

The first step in pricing your item on eBay is to research what similar items have sold for in the past. This information is available through eBay's sold listings feature, which allows you to view the final sale prices of completed sales for specific items.

To access this information, search for your item on eBay and then select the "sold listings" filter on the left-hand side of the search results page. This will show you a list of all the completed auctions for that item and the final sale price.

Pay attention to the selling price of items similar in condition and quality to yours. You can use this information to determine a starting price for your item and set a minimum price you're willing to accept.

Step 2: Consider your item's condition and uniqueness

When pricing your item on eBay, it's essential to consider its condition and uniqueness. Items in excellent condition or that are rare and hard to find may be priced higher than similar items in poor condition or more commonly available.

Take some time to evaluate the condition of your item and compare it to similar articles sold on eBay. For example, if you have the original accessories, original box, and paperwork of your thing, you can price it higher.

Step 3: Choose a median price

Once you've researched and considered your item's condition and uniqueness, it's time to choose a median price that balances getting the best-selling price with attracting potential buyers.

One strategy is to set your starting price slightly higher than the median price of similar sold items. This can help you maximize your profits if there is high demand for your item while giving you room to negotiate and accept offers.

Another strategy is to set your starting price slightly lower than the median price of similar sold items. This can help you attract potential buyers and generate more interest in your article, although it may result in a lower final selling price. Use this strategy when your cost of goods is really low.

Step 4: Monitor your listing

Finally, monitoring your eBay listing closely ensures that your pricing strategy works. You may need to adjust your price if you're not receiving any interest or offers on your item.

On the other hand, if you're receiving multiple offers and interest in your item is high, consider raising your price to maximize your profits.

Pricing your item to sell on eBay requires research, careful consideration of your item's condition and uniqueness, and the ability to choose a median price that balances your desire for a high selling price with the need to attract potential buyers. By following these steps and monitoring your listing closely, you can increase your chances of a successful sale on eBay.

Let's look at an example:

Continuing with the "Fisher Price Little People House," we researched in the previous chapter. We found that this item is desirable and will sell within a short time frame. Let's look at how much this item sold for; this will give us an idea of how to price our item.

Based on the results, our item is similar to the one in the middle, the "Vintage Sesame Street House." The average price for this house sold for 45 dollars. I would list mine a bit higher, say $49, and take offers.

Note: The seller took an offer when there was a line through the sold price. We don't know the offer, but it was less than the original sales price.

As we can see, the price varies depending on the model of house you have, the condition, the accessories it brings, and when the item was made. With toys, the older, the more desirable and valuable.

You have to find one (or a few) items comparable to yours that have sold and use that sold price as a guideline. If your thing is in better condition, has more accessories, etc. You would price your item higher than your competition (pricing your extra pieces individually would give you a total selling price you can start with.)

This starting price should take into consideration offers. So, for this Fisher Price example, let's say you price your house at $47.99, slightly higher than the average price we saw above. However, you set your listing to accept offers.

At that starting price, you should get offers in the low to mid-40s. Offers in the 30-dollar range should only be considered if the item has been sitting for a while, your cost was very low, so you will still make a profit or you want a quick sale.

When pricing, which can be more of an art than a science, you get better with experience. As you research, list, and sell more items. You will become much better at pricing your items because you already did the work and have gained experience.

Do not get intimidated by this process and all the math. Once you become more experienced with your items, you will be able to make this calculation in your head very quickly.

Three Important Things When Pricing your Items:

1. Cost of Goods Sold (COGS)

Keeping your costs as low as possible is crucial to success in this business. You want to have room in your profit for discounts and offers. If the item's price tanks in the market or people stop buying it, you may be left with a dud (a thing that will not sell).

You want to be able to discount it enough to break even, recoup your cost, and move on to better items. So always know what you pay for your inventory.

2. Shipping Costs

You also need to know the shipping cost of your item. For example, everything under 16 ounces will ship First Class mail (in the USA), which will be about $6.45 (as of March. 2023).

Anything heavier than 16 oz will cost $8 and up. As you pick up items to sell, you ship more. You will become familiar with the different shipping rates based on the item's weight.

For example, if you buy a doll to sell, and the doll is 3 pounds. You will know to ship that doll across the country will take $12-$14. So, you will add this amount to your price calculation (if you are doing free shipping, you will include this in your price).

3. **eBay fees**

Having a good understanding of how eBay's fees work is pivotal in succeeding in your business. Luckily, eBay has a nifty calculator that you can use to calculate your fees ahead of time. There is a link at the end of the book.

As of March 2023, eBay fees for most categories are 13.25% plus $.30 per sale. Refer to the eBays Fees chapter in the book for more information on eBay fees.

When pricing your items, a reasonable estimate of your overall costs before you sell an item is necessary. You need to know how much your profit will be.

Use this formula to calculate your total cost of an item:

Cost of item + Fees + Shipping costs = Total Cost.

Then you calculate profit:

Total Cost - (subtract) Sales Price of your item = Profit

Once you get experience selling a few items and shipping, you can do this calculation in your head quickly, especially with those items that weigh less than a pound, since this cost is easy to forecast.

Using eBay Price Recommendations

When listing your items, eBay will give you an estimate of the item's sale price based on its algorithm and data. Although it is an excellent place to start, these recommendations are only sometimes perfect.

Please do your research when it comes to pricing. Not only will you get practice and knowledge on different items, but you can also learn how other sellers price their items. With a little bit of research and some trial and error, you'll be able to find the perfect price point that works for you and your customers.

Pricing is based on your Listing Format.

The strategy to price your items will also vary depending on how you list them, either as an Auction or with a Fixed Price listing as "Buy It Now."

Auction Listings

You want to list items as an Auction if they are unique and in high demand. For example, if the new PlayStation 5 is coming out and you have one or more to sell. Setting up an auction is a good idea because there is little inventory and high demand.

With this approach, the market determines the sales price for your item, not you. You set the starting price low to get noticed, and as the closing date gets near, you should start getting bids.

If you want to ensure you get at least a certain amount for your item, you can set a Reserve Price. You are willing to accept this minimum amount for your item; if the bids do not reach this number, the auction will not sell the item.

You can also set your auction with a Buy it Now price. This option carries an additional fee, but if somebody doesn't want to wait for the auction to end, they can buy it immediately.

This is a great way to give your buyer more options and help them buy from you. You want to use all the tools to ensure your sales stay consistent and your eBay store succeeds.

Fixed Price Listings or Buy it Now

You want to start all your listings as Buy it Now unless, as stated above, you have a highly sought-after unique item with very little supply.

Once you have researched how much your item is selling for, start your listing slightly higher than the competition, and add the best offer.

Once your listing gets traffic, you should get some watchers and interest. If your photos are great, your description is complete, and your price is right, you should start receiving some offers.

Tuning on offers on your listings is excellent because it gives the buyer more options to buy your item. Use all tools available to you.

When To Take Offers on Your Items

When evaluating offers for your item, consider your cost and how long you had that item in inventory.

Many will offer much less than your listing price, which is ok. You do not have to accept it. However, it would be best to always counteroffer with an amount you think is fair. I have often sold items when I counter with just a slightly higher counteroffer.

However, there are times you should consider taking an offer as is. For example, if you have had this item for a long time, and the offer covers at least your cost and fees, go ahead and take what you can.

It's better to take a loss or break even than to sit on items for months or years.

Free Shipping or Charge for Shipping?

When listing your items on eBay, one of the decisions you must make is whether to offer free shipping or charge for shipping. This can be a tricky decision and requires some careful consideration. Here are some factors to keep in mind:

Benefits of Free Shipping:

1. Attract more buyers: Many buyers prefer listings that offer free shipping because it makes the total cost of the item more transparent and predictable.

2. Increase sales: Offering free shipping can increase the likelihood of a buyer purchasing because they don't have to worry about paying for shipping on top of the item's price.

3. Improve search ranking: eBay's search algorithm considers whether a listing offers free shipping, so including it can help your item appear higher in search results.

4. Encourage multiple purchases: If you offer free shipping, buyers may be more likely to purchase various items from you at once since they don't have to worry about paying for shipping multiple times.

5. Free shipping can help you stand out from competitors not offering it.

Drawbacks of Free Shipping:

- As the seller, you must absorb the shipping cost, which can eat into your profits if not carefully calculated.

- Free shipping may attract buyers looking for a bargain and unwilling to pay full price.

However, it's important to be strategic about offering free shipping to avoid losing money. Consider factors like the weight and size of your item, the cost of shipping, and your profit margin.

Free shipping may not be practical or cost-effective for every item, so weighing the pros and cons before deciding is important.

Charging for Shipping on your Listings

Benefits of Charging for Shipping:

- You can accurately calculate and include the shipping cost in the item price, ensuring you do not lose money on shipping expenses.

- Charging for shipping allows you to offer a discount on the item price, which may attract buyers looking for a deal.

- You can offer different shipping options, such as expedited shipping, which can increase your profits.

Drawbacks of Charging for Shipping:

- Buyers may be deterred by the additional shipping cost, reducing the likelihood of a sale.

- Listings with shipping costs may be ranked lower in search results, making it harder for your item to be seen.

In summary, both options have their benefits and drawbacks, ultimately coming down to your personal preference and strategy. Whatever you decide, it is crucial to be transparent about shipping costs and accurately calculate them to avoid losing money.

Chapter 9.
eBay's Marketing Tools

As an experienced eBay seller, I've learned that to be successful on this platform; it's important to use the right marketing tools to get your listings noticed by potential buyers.

In this chapter, we'll discuss the different eBay marketing tools available to sellers and how to use them to boost your sales and grow your business.

eBay offers a variety of marketing tools that can help sellers increase their visibility on the platform, reach more buyers, and ultimately sell more items. By using these tools strategically, sellers can make their listings stand out from the competition and attract more buyers.

This chapter will break down each eBay marketing tool and explain how it works. We'll also provide tips and best practices for using these tools effectively so that you can get the most out of your eBay selling experience.

Promoted Listings

A marketing tool called "promoted listings" can help you increase the visibility of your products on eBay. When you promote your listings, eBay will make them appear above other search results and throughout the search results on the first pages. Your listings will show a little "sponsored" label to let users know it is an advertisement. In my experience, this label has little to no effect on how buyers interact with my promoted listings.

How to Promote Your Listings

Go to your eBay main page, and click on listings to see all your current listings. Please select the items you want to promote (all are recommended), click promote, decide on a percentage, and that's it.

This is the ad cost percentage or the amount you are prepared to pay eBay when a customer clicks on your promoted listing and makes a purchase. The minimum ad cost rate is 2%, but the higher you set it, the more probable your product will be promoted.

Promoted listings are based on the keywords and categories you select when creating the listing, so choosing relevant keywords and categories is important to maximize visibility to potential buyers.

Additionally, eBay's algorithm will consider your item's sales history, pricing, and relevance to the search query to determine whether to promote your item.

One of the key benefits of using promoted listings is that it can increase visibility and sales for your items, increasing the chances of reaching potential buyers searching for similar items.

Plus, you only pay the ad fee if a buyer clicks on your promoted listing and makes a purchase, which can be a cost-effective way to drive sales to your eBay store.

Tips for Promoted Listings:

- Use relevant keywords: When creating your promoted listings campaign, use relevant keywords in your listing titles and descriptions. This will help your items appear in more search results and attract potential buyers.

- Set a competitive ad rate: eBay will recommend an ad rate for your promoted listings based on the competition for your chosen keywords. Consider setting a slightly higher or lower ad rate than eBay's recommendation to see what works best for your items.

- Use high-quality photos: Use high-quality photos in your listings to make your items stand out and attract more potential buyers.

Promotions and Sale Markdowns

The Sales Markdown tool is another excellent option for running sales and promotions on your eBay store. By taking advantage of these tools, you can entice more buyers to purchase your items and ultimately increase your profits.

Here are some tips for running sales and promotions on eBay:

- Plan your sale: It's important to plan your sale to ensure it aligns with your business goals and inventory levels. Consider what type of discount you want to offer and when you want to run the promotion.

- Choose the right items to promote: Not all items are created equal, so be strategic in selecting which items to promote. Look for items with high demand, good profit margins, or items that have been sitting in your inventory for a while.

- Use the correct type of promotion: eBay offers several promotions, such as a percentage-off discount, free shipping, or buy-one-get-one deals. Choose the type of promotion that will appeal most to your target buyers.

- Share your promotion on social media: Promote your sale on social media platforms like Twitter, Facebook, and Instagram to reach a wider audience.

- Set a clear end date: Make sure to set a clear end date for your promotion, so buyers know when the sale will end. This sense of urgency can encourage buyers to purchase sooner rather than later.

- Monitor your sales and adjust as needed: Keep an eye on your sales and adjust your promotion. Try a different promotion or adjust the discount amount if one isn't working.

- Consider offering bundled deals: Offering bundled deals, such as buy-two-get-one-free, can be a great way to encourage buyers to purchase more items from your store.

- Use eBay's email marketing tool: eBay offers a free email marketing tool that allows you to send promotional emails to your eBay subscribers. This tool will notify subscribers about your sale and drive more traffic to your listings.

Here is how to Setup your Promotions:

Go to your Seller Hub page, hover over Marketing (towards the middle of the page), and select Promotions.

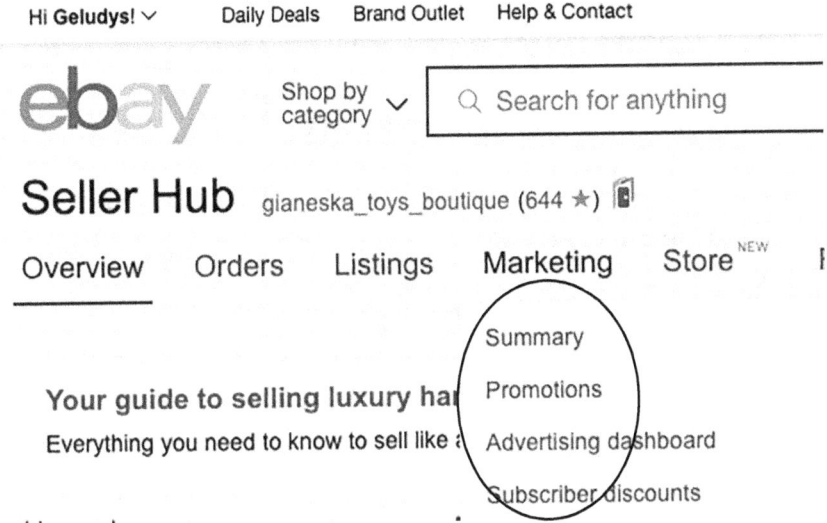

On the right side of the screen, click on the blue button "Create Promotion."

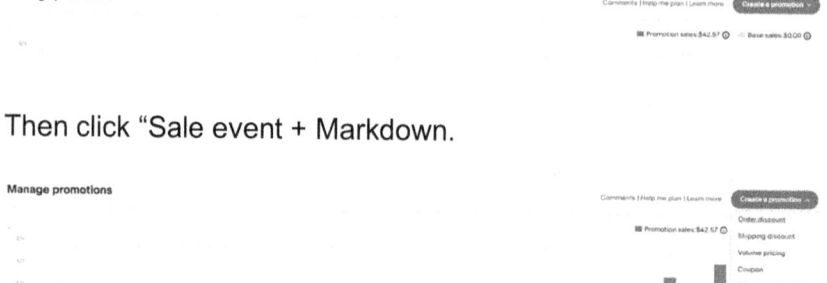

Then click "Sale event + Markdown.

This is where you are going to set up your sale. The process is pretty straightforward.

1. Select the discount percentage

2. Select the items you want to put up for sale

3. Input the date range you want your sale to run

4. Name your sale, and you are done.

Your sale items will reflect the discount and the new discounted price in a few minutes. Your items will now receive a boost in search results.

It has yet to be proven officially, but I have seen my items get an increase in views and watchers as soon as I run a sale. This is because eBay shows discounted items first when a customer searches. Do your test with your times and see if this works for you.

Some tips when running Markdown Sales:

- Figuring out the correct percentage to offer with your sale will be trial and error. You will have to run different sales on different discount percentages until you find the one that will yield the best results.

I noticed they were not increasing my profits when I started running sales. Sometimes I would not get a single sale or many views on my items while the sale was running.

That's when I decided to try and increase my percentage discount. So instead of offering a 10% off sale, I started offering 15 - 25% off, and my sales took off. Now I understand what my customers are looking for regarding a discount.

- Put on sale items that have been in the store for a while and discounted them just enough to make a little after costs. Always ensure I am at least breaking even after heavily discounting the items.

- Start your sale on a Thursday morning, and end it on Sunday at the end of the day. Running a limited-time sale on the weekend has been one of my best strategies so far regarding running promotions.

I have found that people will watch something on sale on Friday and purchase it on Sunday before it ends.

Creating a sense of urgency with the timing, adding a good discount amount (over 15% is advisable), and you can have a winning combination.

- If your item is rare and expensive, sometimes those items will take longer to sell. They have a cycle where buyers watch them for several days (or weeks) before deciding. Have patience for the right buyer, and only discount as a last resort.

Marketing Calendar

I recommend you follow this Marketing calendar for the week (keep it simple):

Tuesday: Send offers to watchers.

Once your items start getting attention and you see some interest, let the item run a bit more and let the interest accumulate.

Send offers when you have more than five watchers and your listing has been active for at least ten days. You only have one chance, so make it count.

Thursday: Set up 10-day auctions for items that need to be liquidated. When you start an auction on a Thursday, your listing will have two full weekends in front of many potential buyers, who do most of their shopping on the weekends.

This turns into much more exposure and a better chance you will find your buyer. Suppose you have made a bad buy or have items sitting with no interest. Start an auction on them. Start the price with the minimum amount that you are willing to get.

eBay will give you a temporary boost at the beginning of the listing period, and you should get some interest. Let the auction run; hopefully, somebody will bid on your item. If there are no buyers, run it again.

I have found that sometimes the right buyer will miss the listing, and if you rerun it, you can increase your chance that they will see it and purchase it. If you run this cycle and still have no bites, I suggest donating it or giving it to somebody who can use it.

Nothing is more depressing than watching inventory sit unsold for months or years. We will buy stuff that will not sell; that's just the nature of this business. The key is to keep it moving, learn from it, and keep moving some more.

Friday to Sunday night: Run your discount promotion sale.

Discount items that have been sitting in your store for a while without any watchers or many views. Having old stale listings can drag your store down in the search results.

Discount those items that are not getting many views or watchers to see if you get some interest. Remember to review your listing to ensure you have chosen the right keywords, your pictures look good, and your price is fair.

Use Item Specifics to Promote Your Listing

One great (and Free!) method to increase your item's visibility is to ensure they are correctly identified. When creating your listing, fill in as many item specifics as possible. This helps the eBay algorithm deliver your item to more people looking for similar items.

You will be more likely to be found if you ensure eBay can index your item correctly. You're telling eBay precisely what your item is, who it is for, and what your price is. Therefore, giving buyers exactly what they want.

Also, you can get a boost on the search results (appear at the top of the page) if your competition fails to fill out their item specifics. Giving you the advantage of being seen by more potential buyers.

By using these tips and ensuring that your item specifics are accurate and complete, you can help the eBay algorithm identify your item and show it to potential buyers, ultimately leading to more sales.

How to Use Social Media to Increase Sales

We live in a world connected by the use of social media. People love to share what they buy and want to buy. Use this to your advantage to promote your business.

Here are some tips to help you plan your social media strategy:

Be Real.

Build trust and credibility by staying true to yourself and not pretending to be someone you're not.

Do not be tempted to post fake sales and fake profits. People can see right through that, be humble. Share your successes and failures and what you learned from them. That is how you build a loyal following. Give more than you take. Consider your audience and how you can make a relationship with them.

Do Not Mix Your Personal Account With Your Business.

Create separate social media accounts and profiles for your business. Not only will you look more professional, but you will be able to interact with your brand, therefore creating brand awareness and building a following.

Start With One Channel And Build From There.

If you are more familiar with Facebook, for example, start there to build your audience. Focus your efforts on one platform at a time.

Do not expect to be an internet sensation overnight. Building the right audience will take time. Just create content that your audience can resonate with, can learn from, and will relate to their lives. More and more people will find your content over time and follow you.

Listen To Your Audience.

Engage with your followers and start conversations. Listen to their concerns and what they like and don't like. Listen to what they are saying about you and others.

Ask questions relevant to your niche, and share their content as long as it's relevant and appropriate.

Consistency.

One of the keys to social media marketing is consistency.

Create a plan to have good content written several times a week. Your followers will expect fresh content from you regularly. You can schedule social media posts ahead of time by using software (google search) or by simply picking a few times a week when you will share something online that is useful to your followers. (Use a planner)

Create Quality Content That Your Followers Will Love

The content can range from tips to make their life easier, life hacks, review products, a day in the life of…, news related to your niche, etc. Make it genuine and quality and your followers will thank you for it by following you.

Encourage Your Followers To Comment And Share Your Content.

Make it useful, make it relevant, and make it accessible. People love to share posts that are useful, wholesome, and relevant. Make it funny and exciting!

Run Contests On Your Social Media Page.

Customers love free stuff! Create a buzz for your store by creating fun contests that your followers can participate in. Make it one of the rules to share your page with their followers—a great way to grow your social media presence and get some sales.

Social media is beyond the scope of this book. If you want to learn more, find a good book written by an experienced source, and learn about using social media to grow your business.

Chapter 10.
How to Cancel a Sale on eBay

Online Grocery

Sometimes, even with the best intentions, you may find yourself in a situation where you must cancel a sale on eBay. This can happen for various reasons, such as the item being damaged or lost in transit, the buyer requesting a cancellation, or you realize that you can no longer fulfill the order.

In these cases, knowing how to cancel a sale on eBay and handle the situation professionally is important.

When to Cancel a Sale on eBay:

- The item is damaged or lost in transit

- You cannot fulfill the order due to an unforeseen circumstance

- The buyer requests a cancellation

- The buyer's payment was not received or processed correctly

- The buyer's shipping address is invalid or incomplete

- You made a mistake in the listing, such as pricing or item details

If you find yourself in any of these situations, acting quickly and communicating with the buyer as soon as possible is important.

Here are some tips for handling cancellations with buyers:

1. Keep the communication lines open: Let the buyer know the reason for the cancellation and apologize for any inconvenience caused. Provide prompt responses to their messages and keep them informed throughout the process.

2. Follow eBay's cancellation policy: eBay has specific rules and guidelines for canceling sales, so be sure to follow them carefully. This includes refunding the buyer

promptly and canceling the transaction through eBay's platform.

3. Leave feedback for the buyer: If the buyer has already left feedback for the canceled sale, you can respond with a polite and professional message explaining the situation.

4. Offer solutions: If you're canceling the sale because of a problem with the item, offer the buyer a refund or a replacement. If there's a problem with the shipping address, ask the buyer for the correct information and offer to resend the item once you receive it.

5. Be clear and concise: Ensure your messages are easy to understand and provide all the necessary information. Avoid using jargon or technical terms that the buyer might not understand.

Cancel for Non-Payment

In the case that the buyer does not pay after four days and you have sent payment reminders, you have two options:

You can manually cancel the sale. Select the "Non-Payment" reason, and the order will be canceled. Or

Let eBay open an "Unpaid Item" case against the buyer. After the case is open, the buyer will be notified that they have to complete their purchase, or the order will be canceled.

If the buyer ignores this and does not pay, he will have a mark in his account (or ding) for non-payment. After a few of those, eBay may terminate the buyer's account.

On the 5th day, if there is still no payment, you must close the case to receive a fee credit for the sale. If you do not complete the case, the buyer's unpaid claim will not be recorded in their account.

You can automate this process by activating the: "Unpaid Item Assistant."

The assistant will:

- Automatically open a case against the buyer after two days of non-payment.

- Close the case once payment is made.

- Close the case after four days of non-payment.

- Relist your item after four days.

- Record the case in the buyer's account (after a few of these, they can be restricted from buying on eBay).

- Close the case and issue your fee credit automatically.

You can opt-in to this service by entering your seller account ⇒ seller preferences.

Returns and cancellations are just another part of this business. Use the tools available to you, and ensure you handle each transaction professionally.

Ultimately, staying calm and responsive is the key to dealing with customer disputes on eBay. By keeping the lines of communication open and working to resolve the issue, you can minimize the impact on your business and maintain a positive reputation on the platform.

Chapter 11.
All About eBay Fees

Imagine you decide to open a store to sell all kinds of socks. What would be the usual way to do it? You'll have to rent a space, get a business license, and outfit the store with display cases, cash registers, etc. You will have to source much inventory to fill your shelves. Maybe hire an employee and invest in advertising.

Well, that's precisely what happens when you open an eBay store, only that you do it in the virtual world instead of the physical—still the same concept. You have the stuff to sell; you want customers to buy. And just like any other business, selling on eBay has expenses.

eBay Fees Breakdown

Insertion Fees

Once you get some sales with your new account and receive positive feedback, eBay will provide you with 250 free listings regardless of whether you have a store. You can get 350 free listings with the starter store if you have a store. Higher-priced stores offer many more free listings.

After you have used your free listings, insertion fees are non-refundable, even if your item doesn't sell:

USD$0.35 per listing (as of March. 2023)

Good 'til Canceled Listings

These types of listings are included in your free listing allowance. These are fixed-priced (not auctions) and will renew automatically every month after they are listed.

After you use your free listing allowance, the insertion fee applies (USD$0.35) and will be charged when you first list the item and each time the listing renews (if you don't have free listings left at that time).

Final Value Fees

eBay charges a final value fee (FVF) for every item sold. The FVF is a percentage of the total amount paid by the buyer, including the item price and any shipping and taxes.

As of March 2023, the FVF for most categories is 13.25% + USD$0.30 per order. The extra $0.30 is charged to cover the cost of processing the payment and submitting taxes to the authorities on your behalf.

For example, if you sold an item for $100 and the FVF was 13.25% + 0.30, you would pay eBay $13.55.

It's important to note that eBay does not charge a listing fee for most items but instead collects the FVF once the item is sold. This means sellers can list as many things as they want without incurring any upfront charges.

Regarding taxes, eBay's "Managed Payments" handles all sales transactions, including tax collection and reporting. If you are a seller on eBay or any other platform, you may be required to collect sales tax from buyers in certain states or countries.

eBay's Managed Payments system will automatically calculate and collect any applicable taxes from buyers and then remit them to the appropriate tax authorities on your behalf. As a seller, you don't need to worry about the complicated tax collection and reporting process, as eBay takes care of it.

eBay Store Subscription fees

When you first subscribe to a store on eBay, you will be charged a prorated fee depending on what day of the month you subscribe. For example, if you sign up for the monthly subscription on April 22, you will be charged from April 22 to April 30. You will be charged again on May 1st for your entire month.

Your store subscription charges will be deducted from any payouts you are due and from any future ones. If you need additional funds to cover this charge, the fee will be deducted from the debit card or bank account linked to your payments account.

It's important to note that eBay subscription fees are charged monthly and automatically renew at the end of each billing cycle unless you cancel your subscription. If you cancel your subscription before the end of the billing cycle, you'll still have access to the benefits until the end of the current cycle.

Here is the link for more information on how eBay charges for their subscription stores: https://pages.ebay.com/stores/subscriptionterms.html

How to Lower your eBay fees:

When you start to sell on eBay, fees can add up quickly. Fortunately, several ways exist to lower your eBay fees and save money.

Here are some tips to help you do just that:

- Check your eBay statement: The first step in lowering your fees is to review your eBay statement carefully. Look for any things that could be corrected, such as incorrect charges or duplicate payments. If you spot any errors, contact eBay's customer support to have them corrected.

- Become a Top-Rated Seller: eBay rewards sellers who consistently provide excellent service with lower fees. To become a Top-Rated Seller, you must maintain a

98% positive feedback rating, offer fast and free shipping, and provide exceptional customer service.

- Sign up for a store subscription: If you're a high-volume seller, it may be worth signing up for an eBay store subscription. Not only does this give you access to additional selling tools, but it also comes with lower fees. The Basic Store subscription, for example, offers lower final value fees and reduced insertion fees.

- Optimize your listings: Another way to lower your eBay fees is to optimize your listings. This means using relevant keywords in your titles and descriptions, using high-quality images, and offering competitive prices. By doing this, you'll increase the visibility of your listings and attract more buyers, which can lead to more sales and lower fees.

- Take advantage of eBay promotions: eBay frequently offers promotions to help sellers save money on fees. These may include free listings, reduced final value fees, or other incentives. Be sure to regularly check your eBay dashboard for these promotions and take advantage of them when available.

- Offer combined shipping: If you sell multiple items to the same buyer, offer combined shipping to save on shipping costs. This benefits the buyer and reduces your fees since you'll only pay for shipping once.

- Opt for longer listing durations: You can save money on listing fees by opting for longer listing durations, such as 30 or 60 days. eBay charges a lower insertion fee for longer-duration listings than shorter ones, which can help reduce your overall fees.

- Use eBay's Global Shipping Program: If you sell internationally, consider using eBay's Global Shipping Program (GSP). This program allows you to ship your items to eBay's shipping center in the US, and eBay takes care of the rest, including customs and duties. While this service has an additional fee for the buyer, it can help simplify international shipping and reduce the risk of unexpected fees.

In conclusion, knowing the fees associated with selling on eBay is important. While they can eat into your profits, there are ways to minimize them and maximize your sales. Remember to factor in these fees when pricing your items, and consider using eBay's shipping discounts to save money on postage.

It's also worth noting that every business has expenses, and eBay is no exception. However, compared to the costs of running a brick-and-mortar store, eBay fees can be relatively low. Plus, eBay offers many tools and resources to help sellers succeed, from marketing and advertising tools to helpful seller support.

Ultimately, success on eBay comes down to providing a great customer experience, offering high-quality products, and using all of the available tools and resources to your advantage.

By staying updated with eBay's policies and guidelines, optimizing your listings with item specifics and other relevant details, and making smart choices regarding pricing and fees, you can build a successful eBay business and enjoy the many benefits of selling on this popular platform.

Chapter 12.
Returns and Refunds

Online Order

Handling returns and refunds can be a challenging aspect of selling on eBay, but it's important to do so in a way that satisfies both you and your customers. Here are some tips for evaluating customer returns and refunds:

1. Know eBay's return policy: eBay has a standard return policy that all sellers must follow. Familiarize yourself with this policy and understand the guidelines for returning items.

2. Determine the reason for the return: When a customer requests a return, it's important to determine the reason.

    Was the item damaged during shipping? Did the customer receive the wrong item? Understanding the reason for the return can help you handle the situation appropriately.

3. Consider offering a partial refund: In some cases, offering a partial refund can be a good solution. For example, if the item was damaged during shipping but is still usable, you might offer a partial refund to cover the cost of any repairs the customer needs to make.

4. Respond promptly to return requests: When a customer requests a return, it's important to respond promptly. eBay has guidelines for how quickly sellers must respond to return requests, so ensure you stay within these guidelines.

5. Provide instructions for returns: Make sure your instructions are clear and easy to follow. Include any necessary forms or labels, and ensure the customer knows who pays return shipping costs.

6. Communicate with the customer: Keep the customer informed throughout the return process. Let them know

when you've received the returned item, issued a refund, and any other relevant updates.

7. Keep records of all communication and transactions. This includes tracking numbers, shipping receipts, and any messages or emails exchanged between you and the customer. These records can help support your case if the dispute needs to be escalated.

Reasons For Returns

1. **"Item Not as Described" (INAD).** This means that the item sent was wrong, arrived damaged, or doesn't match what you described in the listing.

    The eBay Money Back Guarantee Policy covers the customer in this case. Even if you have a "No Return" policy, eBay will approve this return because of the reason.

    You must respond to this return request, or eBay will decide for you and refund the customer out of your funds. eBay will send the buyer a return label to return the item to you (you will be charged out of your sales or bank account for this charge).

    Once you receive the item back, you will have two days to inspect the item returned. If the item that you sold was new, and what the buyer sent was used, opened, and damaged. You may be eligible to issue a partial refund instead of a full one and sometimes, depending on the case, not return anything.

    In this case, you have to contact eBay, and they will decide based on the evidence. Take pictures of the packaging, the item received, and any communication you had with the buyer.

However, if the returned item was in the same condition you sent it, and somehow you missed a flaw or malfunctioned, issue a full refund, including any shipping charges paid.

2. **The buyer decided they do not want the item (Buyer's remorse), and you do accept returns:**

Accept the return: The buyer is responsible for shipping charges to return the item. Once the item is returned, you refund the customer (minus shipping costs).

You will have two days to inspect the item and contact the buyer with any questions. The same applies if the item arrives damaged or in a different condition. You can contact eBay, and they will authorize a partial refund to the customer instead of the total amount.

3. **The buyer decided they do not want the item (Buyer's remorse), and you do NOT accept returns:**

Depending on the case, you can choose not to accept the return and let eBay handle it directly with the customer. You will have to contact eBay and explain your return policy, and they will advise you, depending on the case, how to proceed. Many times, eBay will compensate both the buyer and you for sale. Again, it depends on the issue.

Make sure it is stated in your listing that you do not accept returns. There is a section in the listing flow where you can include your return policy, but also you should put it in your description that you do not accept returns.

If you decide out of good faith to accept the return anyway, the buyer should be responsible for the return shipping costs and should return the item in its original condition. A partial refund policy applies here too.

Return Options

- **Full Refund with no return**

  It is customary to issue a full refund for low-cost items without the customer returning them. Sometimes the cost of having an item returned to you does not make sense.

  For example, you sell something for $15 with free shipping. The buyer received the item, which was different from what was described in the listing. You should have cleaned it or tested it. Now the item is defective, and the buyer wants to return it. Getting the thing back will cost you another $6 in postage.

  Is it worth spending more money to resell a $10 item? You are better off refunding in full, learning from the experience so it does not happen again, and moving on.

- **Offer a Partial Refund**

  In some instances, a partial refund will resolve the customer's issue. Communicate with your buyer to reach a mutual agreement, and ask eBay to step in if you need to.

- **Offer a Replacement or Exchange**

  Sometimes, you can offer to exchange or replace the item purchased. If you have more quantity of the item or a comparable replacement, you can offer the buyer a replacement item. Communicate with your buyer to come to this decision.

  Whatever you do in a return request, always make sure that you conduct yourself professionally, keep emotions aside, and look at the customer request fairly and courteously.

  However, feel free to contact eBay if things get difficult.

Additional Tips For Handling Returns And Refunds

- Consider offering a return policy that exceeds eBay's requirements. This can make your listings more attractive to customers.

- Make sure you're accurately describing the items in your listings. This can help prevent misunderstandings that lead to returns.

- Be proactive about addressing customer concerns. If a customer contacts you with a problem, respond quickly and work to resolve the issue to their satisfaction.

Handling returns and refunds on eBay can be a challenge, but it is essential to providing excellent customer service and building a successful business. By following the tips and best practices outlined in this book chapter, you can ensure that your customers are satisfied with their purchases and feel confident in their decision to do business with you.

Remember to always communicate with your customers in a friendly and professional manner and to be transparent about your policies and procedures. Offer refunds and returns when necessary, but also consider setting clear guidelines and timeframes to avoid system abuse.

By prioritizing customer satisfaction, you can establish a positive reputation on eBay, leading to repeat business and referrals. Don't let the fear of returns and refunds hold you back from selling on eBay – with the right approach, you can manage them effectively and grow your business.

Chapter 13.
How to Keep Financial Records

Starting a new business can be exciting and rewarding but requires hard work, dedication, and organization. Keeping accurate financial records is one of the most important aspects of running a successful business.

This chapter will guide what financial records to keep, how to keep them, and why it is essential for your new eBay business.

What Records to Keep

- **Income**: Keep track of all payments received. Every month eBay will send you a statement. Review it for accuracy and familiarize yourself with how eBay charges you fees. Look for any mistakes or overcharges.

Print it and, store it away in a folder, label it with the current year. Knowing where your income comes from and how much you earn is essential.

- **Expenses**: Keep track of all fees, including storage rent, utilities, inventory, shipping, supplies, and any other costs associated with running your business. This will help you identify areas where you can cut costs and improve your bottom line.

- **Invoices and Receipts**: Keep all invoices and receipts for purchases, sales, and expenses. This will help you verify your expenses and income for tax purposes and other financial reporting.

- **Bank Statements**: Keep copies of all bank statements and credit card statements. This will help you track your cash flow and monitor discrepancies or errors.

- **Tax Records**: Keep all tax records, including tax returns, tax payments, and any correspondence with the tax authorities. This will help you stay compliant with tax laws and avoid penalties.

How to Keep Financial Records

Financial records can be maintained in several ways, including manual, paper systems, or electronic methods, such as spreadsheets or accounting software. The method you choose depends on the size and complexity of your eBay business and your personal preferences.

Paper-Based Systems: Paper-based systems involve keeping physical copies of invoices, receipts, and other financial documents. This method is simple and inexpensive but can be time-consuming and require some storage space. *Check out the end of the book for my "Sales Tracker Log Book" to help you stay on top of your numbers.*

Spreadsheet Software: Spreadsheet software such as Microsoft Excel or Google Sheets can be used to create and maintain financial records. This method is inexpensive and easy to use. Go to my website, **www.QueenThrift.com**, for a free Google Sheets spreadsheet to keep track of your sales, fees, and profit.

Accounting Software: Accounting software such as QuickBooks, Xero, or FreshBooks can be used to automate financial record-keeping. This method is more expensive but offers many benefits, including time savings, accuracy, and the ability to generate reports and financial statements.

Why it is Important to Keep Financial Records

Tax Regulations: Keeping accurate financial records is essential to comply with tax laws and regulations. You must be able to provide evidence of your income and expenses for tax purposes, and accurate financial information will help you avoid audits and penalties.

Financial Planning: Keeping accurate financial records can help you plan and manage your business finances effectively. You can track your cash flow, identify areas where you can cut costs or increase sales, and make informed decisions about investing in more inventory or equipment.

Legal Compliance: Keeping accurate financial records can help you comply with legal requirements, such as those related to employment, health and safety, and business regulations. These apply if you have employees and a location other than your home where you do business.

Business Valuation: If you decide to sell your business, accurate financial information is essential to assess the value of your business and negotiate a fair price.

As you can see, you do not need to be an accountant to be able to keep good financial records; you have to be an excellent bookkeeper.

By keeping track of your income, expenses, invoices, bank statements, and tax records, you can comply with tax laws and not be surprised in case of an audit.

Chapter 14.
Where to Source for Inventory

Once you get experience running your eBay store, you will want to stock up on more inventory. By now, you probably know what you want to sell or what categories to concentrate on.

So where do you go? Everyone goes to the thrift stores, is that the only place to go? Is that the BEST place to go? Well, the answer lies somewhere in between. Let's look at places to score loads of cheap inventory to resell.

Remember that this list is not absolute; it's just to get you started. Depending on where you live, you may or may not have access to these places.

However, take advantage of your location and the potentially unique items you can source. For example, if you live in an area where it gets really cold, you probably have access to good winter gear, which can be expensive when buying new. Think of extra thick jackets in Nebraska for someone in Florida traveling to Iceland.

How about finding swimsuits and summer gear all year round in Florida? These are sought after, especially off-season. Think about selling to folks in Nebraska traveling to the Bahamas. See how it works?

Some Sources for Inventory

Thrift Stores or Second-Hand Shops

Many people get started in reselling by visiting these types of shops. They find a vintage typewriter, they look it up on eBay, and it turns out it is valued at over $500! The store wants $25 for it. And the rest is history.

Shopping at the thrift shop is pretty straightforward. Navigate to the different sections and look for those unique, colorful, vintage, valuable items people seek.

Tips to help you make the most of Thrift Shop Shopping

- **Have a time goal in mind.**

  Stay away from spending hours and hours in one store. It's easy to get distracted and lose focus. You will end up with a cart full of things that will probably not sell or take a long time to sell.

Think about the sections of the store you want to visit first, and start there. Try to limit yourself to a couple of hours so you will use your time wisely.

- **Make friends with the staff.**

Be polite, say hello, and thank you. You do not have to disclose that you're a reseller; they will probably figure it out anyway. Ask if there is any inventory in the back they may want to get rid of.

A great way to get bulk inventory is to buy some of the stuff you want with some they want to get rid of. Taking the good with the bad is an excellent way to build a relationship; if you manage it well, you can get your hands on incredible inventory.

- **Take advantage of sale days. Rewards points, sales, and discount days**. You will have more competition as more people visit these places on sale days.

However, if you get there early, you can score valuables for low prices. Have a strategy before you go; hit those areas first.

- **Visit thrift stores in small towns**.

These don't get many donations, so they have inventory shipped to them from the surrounding bigger cities. Take advantage of the low traffic to score some great items.

- **Do your research before you buy items to sell.**

  After gathering your possible purchases, gather in a quiet place in the store to sort through what you picked. Get your eBay app out and do some basic research on the items you are unsure about.

  Remember to look for a Sales Through Rate of over 50%. That way, your inventory will rotate every two to three months. Only break this rule if the item is very high-value and you are willing to wait for the right buyer to pay the right price.

- **Get to know your stores.**

  Get a feel for what the different stores are better for. Goodwill, for example, is great for clothing and some electronics. Salvation Army for clothing and furniture. Stores in your area will vary so it pays to get to know them.

- **Look for "out of season" items.**

  Think coats and jackets in the summer and shorts and shirts in the winter. Look for clothing not currently in high demand; those are usually donated towards the end of the season. During the offseason, you can score great deals on expensive outerwear, swimwear, and more.

- **Look out for coupons and special sales throughout the week**. Senior, Student, and Military discounts are usually offered on specific days; find out when they are. If those apply to you, you can save on top of the regular value for the day. Check your stores for details and make a note of them.

- **If your store has a glass case or shelves behind the registers with an inventory**. This is where they keep the most valuable items or easily stolen items. Always check those first. In these protective cases, you will find new electronics, jewelry, expensive sneakers, toys, and more.

Local Auctions

Check your local area for companies running auctions. A simple google search "auctions near me" brought up several sites where I can register, look at, and many times bid on items for pennies on the dollar, right from my computer. The items can sometimes be shipped to you, or you can pick them up after the auction ends.

Other companies have auctions on-site, where you must go to their location and physically look and bid on the merchandise. This is a great way to make connections and inspect what you buy firsthand.

Look for reputable auction houses with some positive reviews and willing to work with you. Many will require a registered business with your city or state. Check your local laws on how to do this.

Liquidation Merchandise Brokers

There are websites as well as local places you can go to buy liquidation pallets. These are only discontinued, overstocked, and returned inventory from major stores. Some items will be new, used, or salvaged (broken, missing pieces, untested, etc.)

They sell these items to companies or brokers specializing in reselling these liquidation pallets to smaller sellers.

This is a tricky way to get inventory; you can pay hundreds or thousands of dollars and get garbage. In some cases, you will probably get a few good items tossed around with mostly broken, useless, and unsellable stuff.

The trick is contacting the right person and buying local if possible. This way, depending on where you live, you can save on the high shipping charge.

If you want to explore this further, do a Google search for "liquidation near me." You will be presented with several options in your local area that you contact. As with auction houses, you will probably be required to show your registered business paperwork.

Another advantage is that you can (in many cases) visit the place of business and inspect the pallet before buying it. If you know what you are looking for, you can make a more educated decision once you are in the warehouse. You can negotiate a better price since you are picking up the pallet. It does not hurt to ask.

Ask for references and read available reviews on any company you plan to do business with. Ensure you are dealing with a reputable source; getting your money back after a scam can be frustrating and challenging. Make sure you are doing business with a trustworthy company.

Wholesale Merchandise

Like Auction Houses and Liquidation, wholesale is another excellent way to get much inventory quicker and cheaper. This is obviously for a more experienced seller since your business needs to be registered, and a lot of money and risk are involved.

Once you can zero in on a category or two, your store will have a much higher chance of succeeding. Consider how you can grow your store. The answer is wholesale.

Getting to this point takes time, work, and skill in forming relationships with wholesalers and distributors. Getting good at this takes time to happen.

Take your time to dominate your foundation first, ensure your business can fund all future decisions (avoid taking on debt), and start researching wholesale sources for your best-selling items.

Estate Sales

This has to be one of my favorite ways to get unique and eclectic inventory for my store. Estate sales are nothing more than a liquidation sale of the contents of a home after the owner is no longer residing there.

There are apps and websites dedicated to listing these sales in your area, do a simple Google search to find them.

Here Are Some Tips For Estate Sales:

- If available, preview what will be on sale from the estate sale's company website. Many will sell items from the sale before they open to the public.

- Attend the first day of the sale, right when they open, to get to the best stuff.

- Make sure you have the correct type of payment. Ask before going if they take credit/debit cards or if it is a "Cash Only" sale. You may even have to dust off the good old checkbook. Be prepared to take advantage of any deal and prepare your payment.

- Almost everything inside the house could be for sale, be bold and ask if anything you are interested in is for sale. Chances are that they are.

- Check the condition of any item you buy. You will not be able to return it and lose your money if you are not careful.

- Refrain from bringing oversized bags to the sale. Just get your wallet and your phone for research. They want to limit the risk of shoplifters in these sales.

- If you want to get the best price, but not necessarily the best items, go to the last day and hours of the sale. Many sale organizers will be more open to offers; some may even let you haul it for free.

- Don't forget to check the bathroom cabinets for vintage perfume, cosmetics, hair care, body lotions, etc. Even with just a few drops left, vintage beauty items can fetch money in the resale market.

- Look for vintage hair care appliances, and test them at the sale if possible.

- Be mindful of the organizers. Refrain from rude comments about the house, the decor, the condition, taste in decoration, etc.

Estate sales commonly result from somebody passing away, and organizers are sometimes family members sorting through personal items that will have an emotional connection. Be kind and mindful of this.

Garage Sales

Like Estate Sales, there are apps and websites where you can find garage sales in your area. This way of sourcing is a hit-and-miss.

People can be selling garbage from their garage, or they can be selling their vintage records collection from the 1970s for pennies. You never know; that is why they are so addicting.

Here Are Some General Tips:

- The early bird gets the worm; no doubt about it here. You may miss out on the best if you are absent when they start. Only sometimes, though, but you can be left out. So, try to arrive early by planning your route the night before.

- Do not wake anybody up in the house. If you arrive at the location and there is still nothing outside, wait or leave for your next one.

- Have cash and small bills on hand. Do not lose a deal because you are out a few dollars, and the seller has no change. Be ready to make those deals yours.

- Feel free to negotiate a package deal. Select all the items you want, then ask for a package deal. Many sellers want to get rid of the stuff, and you can score high-end items cheaply.

- Should you need to transport fragile things, have bags, boxes, and paper. Clear out your car's trunk to ensure enough space for what you may find.

- Don't forget to use your eBay app to research items you're unsure about. If an item is over $10, I will look it up to make sure I can make a profit.

- Please inspect all items carefully, as you cannot return them. Test all electrical items, and ensure you have all the pieces and cords that go with your item. Sellers sometimes forget accessories and things you may need for your item.

- Ask the seller if he has anything inside the house he wants to get rid of. Video games, electronics, and kitchen stuff are all valuable in the resale market. Many times I have asked this question, the seller will go inside and bring me boxes of collectibles from their bedrooms that they want gone.

Once I bought about 200 music CDs from this lovely man. His daughter left home many years ago and just forgot about them. I have made over $1,500 out of that box, and I still have more than half of the CDs to list and sell.

Come back on the last day of the sale or the final hours. The seller will be more open to offers at that point. You may not get the best stuff, but you can still score some good deals.

Sometimes the seller will give you the rest of the stuff for free if you haul it away.

Buy from your Local Marketplace

You can also get great deals on apps catering to your local area. For example, there is Offer Up, Let go, and Facebook Marketplace in the USA. You can find all kinds of great deals if you are diligent and consistent in looking.

If you haven't tried those yet, I suggest you install them on your smartphone and browse the local listings in your area.

Look for people selling things in "lots." I once found a person selling nine pairs of Nike Air Jordan for just USD$60. I sold one pair the next day for USD$160. You have to know what to look for, create alerts for when those items come on the app, and zero in on the deal.

Always have your safety as a priority when picking up in person. Avoid bringing a lot of cash; bring someone with you, and let others know where you are going. Stay safe always.

Here Are Some Tips:

- The same haggling as in garage sales applies here. Feel free to offer less than the sales price and ensure the item's condition is what you expect.

- Make sure you meet in a public place with traffic of people and, better yet, lots of cameras. Places like a Police Station, big box stores (front of the store is best, parking lots tend to have blind spots in cameras), and outdoor restaurants work best. Bring somebody to the meeting if possible.

- Keep your phone number secure by only communicating through the app. nobody needs your phone number unless necessary. Protect your information.

- Beware of fakes. Avoid buying expensive designer items; these are easily faked and becoming harder to authenticate through a picture.

- Set up alerts on the apps so you will be alerted when items or categories of items you are interested in hit the market. You will get a notification on your phone and be the first to score the deal! I have found some of my most excellent profit items by being the first to answer an ad.

Facebook Groups

One new way of sourcing for inventory is Facebook Groups. There are many Buy/Sell & Trade groups on the app. Many are catered to specific categories like clothing, shoes, video games, etc. But many others cater to everything (flea market style), and even specific brands. For example, there are groups to buy and sell items like Coach Bags, Gucci, Zara, Nike, and more.

A simple search for your general category, and you should have plenty of choices of groups to join.

Also, look for local groups in your area; with these, you can save on shipping by just picking it up. There are groups where people sell inventory by the piece, the box, the pallet, at the wholesale level, and more.

Some General Tips:

- Once you sign up for these groups, browse their listings and familiarize yourself with how they work.

- Read their rules, as some are strict on what you can sell and buy from the group. You will get kicked out if you violate the guidelines the owner of the group has set.

- If meeting locally, make sure you stay safe when doing any transaction. Meet in a public place like a big box store or a police station. A place with cameras and people around.

- If paying with PayPal. Pay using the "PayPal Goods and Services" option, not "Family and Friends."

In case of fraud with your transaction, you will only be protected if you use the "Goods and Services" option. Always insist on paying as a business with PayPal. If the seller refuses, take it as a red flag and move on to another deal.

- Clean and disinfect items you buy. If possible, spray them outside with antibacterial spray, and leave them to dry in the sun. Use gloves when handling them before you clean them.

- Check the seller's reviews. Buyers can leave a rating on a seller once they conclude a transaction. Check the reputation of the seller by checking the reviews under their name.

- Never agree to send money first. A common scam is inciting a buyer's urgency by asking for payment upfront, usually through a service like Venmo or Cash App. They will use a fake account to retrieve the money and never show up to complete the transaction. Please don't do it.

- Please inspect the product before paying for it. Ensure it is what you want and the condition you expect.

Sourcing inventory for your eBay store can be a fun and creative process. Don't be afraid to get creative and think outside the box when searching for items to sell. With persistence and some luck, you can find profitable inventory and grow your eBay business.

Chapter 15.
What it Takes to Succeed

"Nobody cares; work harder"
Jocko Willink

Starting a business is an exciting and challenging endeavor. It requires hard work, dedication, and determination to succeed. While some entrepreneurs might believe that having a great idea or a unique product is enough to grow, the truth is that hard work is just as important, if not more so. This chapter will explore why hard work is essential for entrepreneurs and provide some success tips.

Why Hard Work Matters for Entrepreneurs

Entrepreneurship is not for the faint of heart. It is a journey full of ups and downs, challenges, and obstacles that require much effort and resilience. Starting a business is not a sprint, but a marathon, and those not ready to do the work, are likely to fail.

Working hard is essential for entrepreneurs because it enables them to:

- **Build a Solid Foundation**
  Starting a business requires a lot of groundwork, such as conducting market research, creating a business plan, securing funding, and building a network of con-

tacts. Hard work is necessary to complete all these tasks efficiently and effectively. Entrepreneurs who put in the effort to build a solid foundation for their business are more likely to succeed in the long run.

- **Overcome Challenges**
  Starting a business takes a lot of work. There will be setbacks, failures, and unexpected challenges along the way. Entrepreneurs willing to put in the hard work are better equipped to handle these challenges and find ways to overcome them.

- **Improve Skills**
  Entrepreneurship requires diverse skills, such as leadership, communication, negotiation, and problem-solving. Hard work is necessary to develop and improve these skills over time. Entrepreneurs willing to try to learn and grow are likelier to succeed.

- **Build a Strong Work Ethic**
  Starting an eBay business is about more than just listing whatever you can find and hoping someone will buy it. It's also about having the discipline and work ethic to make this business successful.

Tips for Being a Successful Entrepreneur

Being a successful entrepreneur requires more than just hard work. Here are some additional tips to help you on your journey:

Focus on Your Strengths

As an entrepreneur, you must wear many hats and juggle various responsibilities. Focus on your strengths and delegate tasks that you're not good at or don't enjoy doing to others. As you get more sales and invest your profits back into the business, hire a Virtual Assistant to help you with the listing process. You can get that time back to the source for more items or ship more articles per day.

Stay Organized

Starting a business involves many moving parts, and getting overwhelmed is easy. Stay organized using a calendar, to-do lists, and other tools to help you manage your time and tasks efficiently.

Check out my website, **www.QueenThrift.com,** to get your All-in-One Reseller Log Book & Planner. Filled with checklists and log pages to help you stay on top of your business.

Build a Strong Network

Networking is crucial for entrepreneurs. Build a network of contacts that can help you with advice, funding, partnerships, and other opportunities. Make friends with the employees at your local stores and business owners, and let them know what you do and what you buy. You'll be surprised how many times they may offer you items before they hit the sales floor. I have gotten things for free just by asking.

Be Adaptable

The business landscape constantly changes, and entrepreneurs must be adaptable to survive. Be willing to pivot your business model, change your approach, or try something new if your current strategy is not working.

You may need to switch to the Auction model because of the type of items that you sell, which do better as auctions. You may need to offer free shipping or returns to attract more buyers. Roll that cost into your sales price and test it out. You only know once you try it and may get surprising positive results.

As I got more experienced, I could calculate shipping costs more accurately. I started to offer free shipping for any item in my store under one pound (first class rate usually at most $6.76). I just rolled that cost into the price, and everyone was happy. My sales increased, my positive feedback rate increased, and things have been smooth sailing ever since.

Learn From Failure

Failure is inevitable in entrepreneurship. Instead of giving up, learn from your failures, and use them as an opportunity to grow and improve.

You are going to buy things that won't sell. Discount them until you break even, or maybe lose a little bit. You will get experience selling that item, customer feedback, and at least will not be a total loss.

You will also buy the occasional non-working, broken, stinking, beyond-belief item you must throw away. You will know next time to check for damaged parts and smells; lesson learned. (Been there)

Believe in Yourself

Starting a business can be daunting, especially if you have never done it. It's easy to feel overwhelmed and doubt yourself. However, believing in yourself and your abilities is important if you want to succeed as an entrepreneur.

Strengthen Your Confidence

Visualize Success

A visualization is a powerful tool that can help you build confidence and believe in yourself. Take a few minutes every day to visualize yourself succeeding in your business. Picture yourself achieving your goals and overcoming obstacles. Visualization can help you focus on your goals and build confidence in your abilities.

Celebrate Small Wins

Starting a business is a long journey, and it's important to celebrate your small wins along the way. Celebrating your successes, no matter how small, can help you build confidence and believe in yourself. Take time to acknowledge your progress and pat yourself on the back for a well-done job. Please do not wait on others for this; you did it.

Surround Yourself with Positive People

The people you surround yourself with can significantly impact your confidence and well-being. Surround yourself with positive, supportive people who believe in you and your business. They can provide you with encouragement and support when you need it most. Remove toxic relationships that will bring you down.

Take Small Steps

Starting a business can be overwhelming, but taking small steps can help you build momentum and confidence. Break your goals into smaller, more manageable tasks, and focus on completing them individually. Each small step can help you build trust and keep you motivated.

Start with a small listing goal. One to two items a day, and build from there. Do not get overworked early on, and remember to take breaks.

Learn from Your Mistakes

No one is perfect, and everyone makes mistakes. Instead of beating yourself up, use them as opportunities to learn and grow. Analyze what went wrong, and use that information to improve your business and skills. Learning from your mistakes can help you build confidence and sharpen your skills.

Believe in Your Vision

Believing in your vision is critical to building confidence in your business. Your vision is what drives you and your business forward. It's essential to have a clear, compelling vision that you believe in. If you believe in your goals, others will too.

Practice Self-Care

Taking care of yourself is critical to building confidence and staying focused. Make sure you're getting enough sleep, eating well, and taking time to exercise and relax. Taking care of yourself can help you feel more energized and excited, which can help you build confidence in your business.

Starting a business can be challenging, but believing in yourself is critical to success. Use these tips and strategies to build confidence, stay focused, and achieve your business goals.

Remember, you have what it takes to succeed. Believe in yourself and your abilities, and you'll be well on your way to building a successful business.

In Conclusion

Congratulations, you've made it to the end of this book on how to sell on eBay for beginners! You now have the knowledge and tools to start your successful eBay business. It's time to take the leap and turn your dreams into reality.

Starting a new venture can be scary, but don't let that hold you back. Remember, every successful eBay seller was once a beginner, just like you. Take small steps, learn from your mistakes, and don't give up. Selling on eBay is not a get-rich-quick scheme, but you can build a profitable and fulfilling business with hard work and dedication.

As you embark on your eBay journey, always prioritize your customers. Provide excellent customer service, ship your items promptly, and be transparent in your listings. These simple practices will help you build a loyal customer base and earn positive feedback.

Finally, believe in yourself and your ability to succeed. You've already taken the first step by learning about eBay and how to sell on the platform. You can achieve anything you want with patience, persistence, and a positive attitude.

I wish you the best of luck in your eBay selling journey. Remember, you are not alone - countless resources and communities are available to help you along the way. Keep learning, keep growing, and most importantly, have fun!

Here is an overview of How to Sell on eBay:

||||||||||||||||||||||||||||||||||||||||||||||||||||||||||||||||||||||||||||||||||||||||||||||||||||||||||||||||||||||||||||||||||||||

Research the market for the items you want to sell. Gather the necessary information to determine the best pricing for your products.

Create an account on eBay. Make sure to choose a unique user-name and fill out the necessary information.

Set up your payment options. Make sure you have a secure and reliable form of payment to accept payments from all potential buyers.

Take quality photos of the items you plan to sell. Use a clean, well-lit background, take plenty of pictures, and take them from multiple angles.

Write an accurate and detailed description of each item. Include any relevant information about the item's condition and features. Also, any flaws and test results.

Determine the shipping cost for the items. Calculate the cost and include the shipping amount in the listing. Use the eBay shipping calculator in the links section.

Choose the right category for your listing. Select the appropriate category so the right buyers will see your item.

Create a return policy. Include information about returns, refunds, and exchanges in your listing.

Promote your listing. Use the eBay promotion tools.

Provide excellent customer service. Make sure to respond quickly to buyers' questions and inquiries. Under promise and over-deliver.

Pack and ship the items sold. Make sure to use clean and quality materials. Always provide tracking information to buyers.

Leave feedback for the buyers. Make sure to leave positive feedback to keep them coming back.

Stay on top of eBay's policies and guidelines. Ensure you know and comply with eBay's rules to avoid any issues.

Be patient. Selling on eBay may take some time, but with the right strategies and techniques, you can be successful.

Reseller Terminology
(Lingo)

Long Tail

This means that the item could take a long time to sell. Think wedding dresses, snowsuits, high price collectibles, and art. Things that people buy infrequently.

Short Tale

An item that will take a short time to sell because of its demand, seasonality, or scarcity. Things like the PS5, Apple Watch, Apple products in general, new Nike sneaker drops, etc.

Sourcing

Going out shopping for things to sell. Visiting thrift stores, garage sales, liquidation stores, wholesale vendors, storage units, etc.

Bins

Refers to the Goodwill Outlet Stores, where merchandise is piled up in bin-like storage carts. Items are sold by the pound, and usually, there is a large number of people shopping for items to resell there. Many treasures have been found in these places. Google your local area.

Low Ball Offer

Refers to receiving a very low offer on your item. For example, if your sale price is $79, you receive a request for $29. Do not get offended or take it personally (it's business); counteroffer or decline.

Quick Tip: Never get snarky or condescending with a potential buyer over a lowball offer; counter with your best, decline, or ignore.

Sale Through Rate (STR)

The number of units sold/ units available for sale (listed) x 100 You will get the percentage of units sold every 90 days.

Comps or Comparable

This refers to researching the value of an item on the eBay website (or app). See the chapter on Item Research for how to do this.

Death Pile

This refers to unlisted inventory getting piled up. This is a common problem because as you get more and more experience, you start to buy more and more items. The deals are everywhere, and you can't help yourself from all the bargains that come your way.

This death pile can become extremely overwhelming if you don't establish an efficient inventory system early on. So, try never to let it get to this.

BOLO

Be On the Lookout

This refers to items in hot demand, which are very valuable and desirable. Think a special edition of a Barbie doll, a vintage Nike sneaker coming up in value, or a product that went viral for some reason, and now everyone wants it.

Dumpster Diving

This refers to people going to garbage bins behind shopping malls, stores, homes, etc., and looking for items they can resell. There are many YouTube videos where you can watch people doing this and finding brand new items behind stores like Victoria's Secret, Nike, Macy's, and more. However, this can be very illegal, depending on where you live. So if you're going to do this, check with your local law enforcement to ensure you will not get in trouble.

BIN (Buy it Now)

This refers to when you set up your listing instead of setting up an Auction where people have to wait to buy. You set up your listing as "Buy it Now," so anyone can purchase your item anytime.

INAD (Item Not As Described)

This refers to a buyer initiating a return because the item was underrepresented in the listing, which means that the item they received does not match the listing for sale.

This can be a very deceptive practice from buyers since eBay forces all returns because of this reason; many buyers know this. One way to avoid this is by taking detailed pictures of every angle of your item. Ensure you document every piece including tags, markings, signatures, serial numbers, etc. Anything that you think the buyer may initiate a return on? Cover yourself as much as you can.

EUC (Excellent Used Condition)

Only use this expression to describe your item if it is in excellent condition. This means no rips, tears, smells, broken pieces, missing pieces, or not working. Clean and test your items before you list them.

GTC - Good 'til Cancelled

A listing format that allows a seller to list an item for an indefinite period, until it sells or the seller removes the listing.

HTF (Hard to Find)

This one is used on those hard-to-find collectibles. However, I would refrain from using this. It's not a term people use to find stuff, and it makes you sound pretentious and amateurish.

MIB (Mint in Box)

This refers to precious collectibles and their mint boxes. Collectors are very particular about their boxes and will look for those in MINT condition. Only use it if your item is indeed in mint condition.

NRFB (Never Removed From Box)

Just like the name says. This item was never removed from the box.

NWT (New with Tags)

The item is new with original tags attached.

NWOT (New Without Tags)

The item is new, but original tags were removed.

OOAK (One of A Kind)

This refers to those art pieces where only one piece exists—items like custom painted artwork, modified dolls, upcycled clothing, and more.

CROSS LIST

This refers to listing the same item on different platforms. For example, you list the same thing on eBay, Mercari, Poshmark, Etsy, and others. Remember that when an item sells, you must delete them from all other sites. So being organized is critical to avoiding canceling orders.

Useful Links

This is a guide; these links can only change with notice.

eBay Selling fees https://www.ebay.com/help/selling/fees-credits-invoices/selling-fees?id=4364

eBay Store Subscriptions: **https://export.ebay.com/en/marketing/ebay-store/why-get-ebay-store/**

eBay's Item Specifics Page https://pages.ebay.com/seller-center/listing-and- marketing/item-specifics.html

eBay's Shipping Calculator https://www.ebay.com/shp/Calculator

eBay's Prohibited and Restricted items https://**www.ebay.com/help/policies/prohibited-**restricted-items/prohibited-restricted-items?id=4207

Pirate Ship www.PirateShip.com

Check out these other titles by Queen Thrift

Finally, a planner specially made for us resellers!

This is the only planner you will ever need. It is not dated, so you can start whenever you want—enough space to keep track of a year in sales.

Included are instructions and tips to use the worksheets, you will find:

- Business expenses tracker for things like gas, supplies, etc.
- Miles tracker
- Cost of goods sold tracker.
  Knowing how much you are spending on new inventory will help you stop wasting money.
- Monthly sales tracker. Knowing how your sales are doing month by month is crucial to growing your business.
- Weekly goals checklist, stay on track, and make more money!

- Inventory log. helpful to write notes and measurements of items.
- Return log, keep track of returned items for inventory purposes.
- Goals worksheet list for resellers
- Sale days tracker. Know when the items you want will be on sale. Plan your sourcing route to take advantage of sales and discounts!
- BOLO (be on the lookout) worksheet. Keep track of trendy and profitable items in this simple worksheet.

Grab your copy today! Find it on Amazon or at
www.QueenThrift.com

Clothing Reseller Inventory Log Book: Stock Control for Fashion Sellers on Poshmark, eBay, Mercari, or Anywhere!

Finally, an inventory book for us clothing resellers!

The only book you will ever need to keep track of all your items.

How many hours have you spent looking for one or more items in your inventory? How many orders have you had to cancel because you could not find the item?

Stop wasting money and killing your business, get organized!

The less time you spend figuring out where an item is for sale, the more money you make!

Time is money! That is very true!

This ledger will give you a good view in your inventory. With these inventory sheets you can keep track of your items:

- Cost
- Measurements
- Date acquired
- Store acquired
- Flaws
- Condition
- Location

This inventory ledger will keep you organized so you have more time to grow your business.

Grab your copy today!
Find it on Amazon or at
www.QueenThrift.com

Space to keep track of 380 items! Finally, an inventory log book for us online resellers!

The only book you will ever need to keep track of all your items.

This ledger will give you a good view in your inventory. With these inventory sheets you can keep track of your items:

- Cost
- Date acquired
- Store acquired
- Flaws
- Condition
- Location
- Date Sold
- and More

This inventory ledger will keep you organized so you have more time to grow your business.

Grab your copy today! Find it on Amazon or at
www.QueenThrift.com